Conflict and Triumph

Conflict and Triumph

The Argument of the Book of Job Unfolded

William Henry Green

THE BANNER OF TRUTH TRUST

THE BANNER OF TRUTH TRUST
3 Murrayfield Road, Edinburgh EH12 6EL
P. O. Box 621, Carlisle, Pennsylvania 17013, USA

★

© Banner of Truth Trust 1999

First published as *The Argument of the Book of Job Unfolded*
by Robert Carter & Brothers, 1874

First Banner of Truth Edition 1999
ISBN 0 85151 761 7

★

Unless otherwise indicated, all Scripture quotations
are taken from the New King James Version
© 1982 by Thomas Nelson, Inc.

★

Typeset in 12/13 pt Bembo at
The Banner of Truth Trust, Edinburgh
Printed by Bell and Bain Ltd, Glasgow

Cover picture by Daniel Tennant, Bainbridge, New York

Contents

Publisher's Preface

William Henry Green was Professor of Biblical and Oriental Literature at Princeton Theological Seminary from 1851 until 1900 when he died. He was an erudite linguist and most capable exegete, held in awe as a teacher, greatly beloved by his students and colleagues and respected by his adversaries. For some four years he engaged in pastoral ministry and retained a life-long interest in speaking to children.

The closing decades of the nineteenth century saw upheavals in the American Presbyterian Church over the nature of Scripture. Along with A. A. Hodge, B. B. Warfield and others, Green engaged in upholding the plenary inspiration of the Bible. He demonstrated the literary integrity of the Pentateuch over against the Graf-Wellhausen theory of its composition and also argued trenchantly for the accuracy of biblical history in *The Old Testament Canon* (1889), *The Higher Criticism of the Pentateuch* and *The Unity of the Book of Genesis* (1895) and in his *General Introduction to the Old Testament* (1898–9).

In addition to the Pentateuch, the book of Job was the focus of many difficulties and Green faced up to these. Recognizing the book as a literary masterpiece, but also the truth of God, he examined how its various parts integrated with each other in relation to its saving message. The result is this masterly and movingly written overview which we are pleased to republish.

Green showed that the theme of the book is not the problem of suffering but the afflicting of the righteous, and that 'the adversary' of God and of his servants, though awesome, is conquerable, even by a 'saint in the dark', for Job did not know what was really happening to him. In addition, Green showed that God's pursuit of his own glory in Job's life is no more 'self-centred' than Job's worship of him had been, for God did not sacrifice Job's well-being but increased it. Job is seen, while still on the dunghill, praying for his 'friends' who, misled by Satan, had savaged him. Both God and Job, therefore, may be said to gain and win, the former in glory and the latter in piety. Satan is the only self-centred one in the book, and he is crushed, being defeated not only by God but also by Job.

The Trust is grateful to Dr Digby James of Weston Rhyn, Shropshire, for initial work done on this text. Green's words are largely unchanged but the New King James Version is used instead of the 1611 translation.

Author's Preface

It may be worth considering whether current methods of dealing with the Bible do not favour a fragmentary, rather than a comprehensive, knowledge of the sacred volume. The attention given to detached and scattered portions of Scripture should be corrected or supplemented by the careful study of entire books, by him who aspires, as every Christian should, to a thorough acquaintance with the Word of God. It is in the hope of encouraging and aiding such a study of the book of Job that this volume has been prepared.

It is not a continuous commentary, occupying itself with the exposition in detail of each successive paragraph or sentence. Nor is it concerned with the vexed questions of its age or authorship. Its aim is simply to set forth its general drift, to exhibit its plan and structure, and trace the course of thought from first to last by showing the part taken by each of the actors, the purport of their several speeches, and the bearing of each portion of the book upon the common theme of the whole.

Such a comprehensive survey as is here proposed will be an excellent preparation for more detailed study subsequently. And the coherence of parts thus exhibited furnishes the best demonstration of the unity of this remarkable book against those who have ventured to apply to it the critical knife.

The author hopes that this humble effort may be of some service in promoting a better understanding and a higher appreciation of the book of Job, among both ministers and laymen. And he will be particularly happy if any afflicted child of God can be assisted in drawing the waters of consolation from this inspired and copious source.

WILLIAM HENRY GREEN
Princeton, New Jersey
11 October 1873

I

Analysis of the Book of Job

Theme: The Temptation of Job

Introduction, 1:1–5

Job's pious character and happy estate.

First Stage of Temptation, 1:6–22

The loss of his property and children;
Job victorious over the temptation.

Second Stage of Temptation, 2:1–10

The infliction upon his own person;
Job still victorious.

Third Stage of Temptation, 2:11–42:17

The persistence of suffering;
Job's struggle and ultimate deliverance.

Third Stage of Temptation
Preliminary statement, 2:11–13
The coming of Job's three friends.

a. The Struggle, Chapters 3–31
Job's complaint, Chapter 3.

The discourses of Job and his three friends, Chapters 4–31

First Series, Chapters 4–14
Job in unrelieved despair.

Second Series, Chapters 15–21
Job rises from despair to hope, and vanquishes the temptation in his second reply to the second friend.

Third Series, Chapters 22–31
Job silences his friends, but the enigma remains.

b. The Deliverance, Chapters 32–42

Elihu's theoretical solution, Chapters 32–37, which is preliminary to

The LORD's practical solution, or intervention for the rescue of Job, Chapters 38–42

1. Spiritual, 38:1–42:6.
The LORD manifests himself to Job, thereby bringing him to humility and penitence.

2. External, 42:7–17
Job vindicated before his friends, and his former prosperity doubled.

[2]

2

Job's Happy Estate

There was a man in the land of Uz, whose name was Job; and that man was blameless and upright, and one who feared God and shunned evil (Job 1:1).

The book of Job is one of the most remarkable in the Old Testament. Apart from its inspiration, and considered simply as a literary production, it bears the stamp of uncommon genius. It is occupied with a profound and difficult theme, the mystery of divine providence in the sufferings of good men. This is not treated in the abstract, in simple prose or in a plain didactic method. But an actual case is set vividly before the reader, in which the difficulty appears in its most aggravated form.

By an extraordinary accumulation of disasters a man of unexampled piety is suddenly cast down from his prosperity, and reduced to the most pitiable and distressed condition. And then there is delineated in the most masterly manner the impression made on others by the spectacle of these calamities, as well as the inward conflict stirred in the sufferer himself, his bewilderment and sore distress, his alternations of despair and hope, his piteous entreaties for a sympathy which is denied him and his irritation under the unjust suspicions and censures which are cast upon him, his wild and almost passionate complaints against the providence which crushes him, intermingled with expressions of strong confidence in God which he cannot abandon.

This wild tumult in his soul is graphically depicted in its successive stages, until we are brought to the final solution of the whole, and the vindication at once of the providence of God and of his suffering servant. And all this is set forth in the loftiest style of poetry, abounding in fine imagery and containing passages of deep pathos as well as of rare sublimity and power; while the whole presentation and treatment of the case is managed with consummate skill.

The book of Job well deserves the high encomiums which have been bestowed upon it as a product of the poetic art. And while we humbly receive its inspired lessons, there is no reason why we should be insensible to its graceful beauty, or refuse to recognize its other attractions. The Bible is not, indeed, amenable to the laws of criticism, nor to be judged of by ordinary standards of taste. When God speaks to us, we must reverently listen and obey, however homely the medium through which he communicates his will. And yet it adds to the variety of this holy book, and to its adaptation to the needs of all classes of men, and to all the cravings of the human soul, that it addresses itself likewise to the refined taste and the cultivated sense. Like the inexhaustible supplies of nature in its manifold diversity, the volume of divine revelation gives us not only the massive granite and the ponderous metal, but the sparkling and polished gems of thought; not only the staple articles of food, but the rarer and more palatable delicacies. So that the charms and the embellishments of poetic genius, which invest other subjects with such attractions, are lent likewise to the sacred oracles in the sweet lyrics of David, the impassioned fire of Isaiah, and the marvellous beauty of the book of Job.

The principal personage of this book, and the one about whom the interest chiefly centres, is Job himself, a venerable and patriarchal character, whose fortunes are detailed to us at an important crisis of his life. Some have thought that he was not a real, historical person, and that the narrative of the book is not one of events which actually took place, but that it is rather a fiction or a parable like that of the Prodigal Son or the Good Samaritan, and that he is designed to represent not some one person to whom all this happened precisely as is here detailed, but a whole class, such as is often met with in real life, of similar character and similar experiences, and the truth of which lies in its general conformity to what repeatedly takes place, and in the correctness of the lessons conveyed.

This, however, cannot have been the case. It is related, not as a parable, but as a history, instructive throughout, as all the Bible histories are, but still an actual, veritable occurrence. And Job is spoken of in other parts of Scripture as a real person, and in connection with other real persons like Noah and Daniel, and the events of his life are referred to in a manner which implies that they had actually occurred. We can have no doubt, therefore, that, with all the poetic embellishment of the narrative, Job did actually live, and the history took place substantially as it is here related.

In this chapter what is proposed for consideration in the life of Job is his character and condition when he is first introduced to our notice, his great excellence and piety and his happy, prosperous state, as these are sketched briefly, but strongly, in the opening verses of the first chapter, and again in Chapter 29, where, after his gloomy reverses, Job pathetically recalls the joys of former years.

We commonly think of Job as a sufferer; and the lessons that we mostly associate with him are those which concern affliction. His great sorrows form indeed the grand crisis of his life; and it is to their exhibition, together with the attendant principles of God's dealings with him, that this book is chiefly devoted. But the very point of the whole lies in their exceptional character, which requires an explanation. If this were not so, there would be no mystery to be elucidated. The enigma is in the contrast between what Job had to endure and what it might be expected would befall such a man as he; what is, in fact, the ordinary experience of such men, and what had been Job's own experience up to the time when he was overtaken by these extraordinary calamities. 'Godliness is profitable for all things, having promise of the life that now is and of that which is to come.'

This saying was fulfilled in the life of Job which had been one continued course of prosperity and happiness up to the time of his heavy trial. It seemed as though nothing had been left for him to desire. As he himself expresses it:

As *in* the days *when* God watched over me;
When His lamp shone upon my head . . .
When my steps were bathed with cream,
And the rock poured out rivers of oil for me! . . .
My root is spread out to the waters,
And the dew lies all night upon my branch (29:2–3, 6 & 19).

The freshness of a well-watered tree, the richness of cream and oil, the brilliancy of God's own light, are the figures which set forth his joyful and prosperous abundance. And, as the tempter sneeringly said, Job had not feared God for nought. God had made an hedge about him and about his house and about all that he had on every side. He had blessed the work of his hands, and his substance was increased in the land.

While, therefore, we go very properly to Job's dark hours to learn the uses of affliction, and all the salutary lessons which accompany it, it behoves us likewise to remember the lesson of all those years which had preceded, namely that God's blessing attends the righteous.

For
'He who would love life
And see good days,
Let him refrain his tongue from evil,
And his lips from speaking deceit.

Let him turn away from evil and do good;
Let him seek peace and pursue it.
For the eyes of the LORD *are on the righteous,*
And his ears are open to their prayers;
But the face of the LORD *is against those who do evil'*
(*1 Pet.* 3:10-12).

Let us attend, then, to the piety and to the happy estate of Job, with the view of taking note how these are combined in the ordinary providence of God. It is not said that there are no exceptions. There are such exceptions. There are grave and weighty reasons why there should be. Job himself was a notable exception at one epoch in his life. Nevertheless the ordinary rule remains; and in the number and the mystery of the exceptions we must not forget that it is the rule, a rule verified for the most part even in the general tenor of their lives who constitute the most signal exceptions, a rule which found its evident exemplification in the greater portion of the life of Job himself. Goodness and happiness go hand in hand in the ordinary experiences of this world.

Let us review, in the first instance, the simple description here given of the piety of Job. He is evidently portrayed as a model man. God himself says of him, 'There is none like him on the earth.' And in the delineation of Job's piety notice, first, two omissions in the narrative, which in a book belonging to the Old Testament, are highly significant.

The first is that no account is given of Job's ancestry or of his connection with the covenant people of God. There is no mention of his parentage, no hint of his relationship to Abraham. He was plainly not one of his descendants. Now if what secures the favour of God be a pious ancestry, or a connection with the outward visible Church, it is unaccountable that in the case of Job, held up as a model before all ages and generations, and of whom God gives such a testimony as he does of no other, that these things are not so much as once alluded to, even for the sake of explaining their absence or omission. Evidently, it is not outward associations or connections, though of the most sacred kind, that constitute the evidence and pledge of God's favour, but personal character and life. In every nation and in every communion, whoever fears him and works righteousness is accepted by him. The important question is not, 'Are you a Jew or a Gentile? Are you a member of this or that particular branch of God's visible Church?' Nor even, 'Are you a member of any outward body of professing Christians whatever?' but, 'Have you personally that character which is acceptable to God, and are you leading a life that is pleasing in his sight?'

A second omission in the account of Job's piety which is also significant is that it is not described as consisting of ceremonial observances. No mention is made of any round of ritual service, no fasts or purifications or tithes, no rigorous periods of abstinence or self-mortification or ascetic observance, no priestly intervention or sacerdotal absolution, no holy order of men through whom grace was dispensed as its sole appointed channel. The only religious rite referred to is the simple sacrificial worship of patriarchal times, maintained in faith of the sacrifice and the atonement that was to come, and which was afterwards accomplished by the Son of God on Calvary. Job was priest in his own house; his own hands offered the sacrifice, though devoid of the grace of orders, and without priestly consecration, and it was accepted. Job's religion was one of the heart and of the life, not of ritualistic service.

And it is the more striking because this is a model of piety belonging to the Old Testament. It is another illustration of the pains that were taken, even under that restricted and legal economy, to fortify the people against that spirit of bigotry and Phariseeism into which they were so prone to fall, and did fall, and which has in fact been the bane of vital religion in every age. Here was an outstanding and shining example. Job was an eminent saint of God, though his line of descent was not counted from Abraham, and though he did not practise the multiplied rites of the Mosaic ceremonial.

Whatever advantages there may be in an outward connection with the people of God or the visible Church, and whatever benefit may arise from outward attendance upon the services of religion, and certainly neither of these are to be decried or undervalued, when rightly understood and put in their proper place – that piety which has the approbation of God is something different from them and independent of them.

The general description of Job's piety is given briefly and simply in four particulars: he was blameless and upright, and one that feared God, and shunned evil. But this statement, brief as it is, is very comprehensive. 'He was blameless and upright.' Uprightness denotes, in the first place, honesty, straightforwardness, sincerity. There was no double dealing or duplicity, no hypocritical pretence with Job, either towards God or man. He was sincere in his professions and honest in his practice. Uprightness, moreover, means conformity to the standard of right, and this both inwardly and outwardly.

We read both of the upright in heart and of the man that is upright in his way. He was a man of integrity, therefore, both in spirit and in life – a man attentive to his obligations both to God and man, and who punctually discharged them. And, with all, he was blameless (or *perfect*, KJV) – perfect and upright, perfect in his uprightness.

Perfect, not of course in that sense in which, according to the uniform teaching of Scripture, and the universal experience of men, perfection is unattainable in this life. Not that he was absolutely faultless, for there is no man that lives and sins not. Job never claims spotless innocence. He himself says,

Have I sinned?
What have I done to You, O watcher of men? (7:20).

But how can a man be righteous before God?
If one wished to contend with Him,
He could not answer Him one time out of a thousand
(9:2–3).
Though I were righteous, my own mouth would condemn
   me;
Though I *were* blameless, it would prove me perverse (9:20).

But he was perfect in the sense of completeness. His uprightness was not of that partial, limited kind, which restricts itself to certain classes of duties, while neglecting others; or confines itself to special times and occasions, while at others it is laid aside; which is very zealous about some of the commandments, to the disregard of others, tithing it may be the mint, anise, and cummin with scrupulous exactness, while neglecting the weightier matters of the law, or manifesting great devotion on Šabbath days or periods of special religious observance, while the duties of other days are overlooked.

A man who can be devout in Church and dishonest in his business, penitently ask God's forgiveness and yet be unforgiving himself, who can profess great love to the Saviour and yet be heartless to Christ's needy poor, this was not the style of Job's piety. He was perfect as well as upright. There was a completeness in his piety, which compassed the whole round of obligation. He studied conformity to the rule of right in all things, at all times, under all circumstances.

And the spring of this perfectness and uprightness, or this complete integrity, was that he feared God. He set the will of God before him as his rule, the glory of God as his end, the approbation of God as his highest reward. In this pious fear of God he walked all the day long. This was his grand motive, overpowering every thing else. This closed his ear against the siren song of temptation. This shut his eyes to every gilded lure of sin. The one thought, 'You are the God who sees', was his safeguard and his stimulus. This impelled him to prompt and ready obedience to every divine command. This made him steadfast in his uprightness, and led to his perfectness and completeness in it.

It also led to the sedulous avoidance of its opposite, and thus completed the perfect square by the fourth side, which is the finishing stroke to this description of a well-regulated piety. He 'shunned evil': he carefully shunned all sin, kept aloof from everything that was wrong in heart, speech, and behaviour. Some eminently good and holy men have great blemishes; they apparently lay out all their strength on the positive side of religion, and neglect its negative; they endeavour strenuously to do right, and forget to strive against doing wrong. And thus they leave the periphery of the Christian character unfinished: the last side, which completes the whole, and gives it symmetry, is never added. A great gap is left unfilled. There was no such lamentable deficiency in the case of Job. He 'was blameless and upright, one who feared God and shunned evil'.

Besides this general description of Job's pious integrity, two special traits are incidentally mentioned in different parts of the book, by which he was particularly characterized, and which belonged to him in separate walks of life. Not as though these were by any means the only ways in which his piety manifested itself. But they were marked and prominent, and they may serve as illustrations of his habitual piety and consistency in two several spheres; viz., at home and abroad, in the intimacies of the domestic circle and in his intercourse with others less nearly related to him.

In regard to the former, mention is made of a fact which serves to show Job's pious regard for the spiritual welfare of his children. It was the sacred habit of the family to throw the safeguards of religion around every period of mutual entertainment and social enjoyment. Whenever his children gathered, as they regularly did, at each other's houses on festive occasions, cementing and displaying their fond fraternal affection, it was Job's invariable custom to summon all together afterwards, and sanctify them, and offer burnt offerings according to the number of them all. For Job said, 'It may be that my sons have sinned and cursed God in their hearts' (1:5).

'Cursed God' is too strong an expression for the meaning intended here. It is not blasphemy, or defiance of God, or malignant hatred of his service that he feared. The word is properly a formula of blessing, used in taking leave of friends. It is commonly translated 'bless', and is the same that is employed where it is said, 'And early in the morning Laban

arose, and kissed his sons and daughters and blessed them'
(*Gen.* 31:55). 'So Joshua blessed them and sent them away'
(*Josh.* 22:6); that is, he took leave of them, he said farewell to
them, he bid them adieu.

Job was afraid that his sons might have said farewell to God
in their hearts; that they might have taken leave of him; that,
in their thoughtless hilarity, they might have forgotten God
and his presence, and acted as though they were out of his
sight. He recalls them to solemn thought and to their
Maker's service, while he solicits the pardon of their sins by
the offering of sacrifices according to the number of them all.

Job's piety manifested itself at home in thoughtful care for
his children's spiritual good. But it was not limited to his own
household. He sought the good of all. And he was especially
forward in the relief of the needy and the protection of the
injured:

> When the ear heard, then it blessed me,
> And when the eye saw, then it approved me;
> Because I delivered the poor who cried out,
> The fatherless and *the one* who had no helper.
> The blessing of a perishing *man* came upon me,
> And I caused the widow's heart to sing for joy . . .
> I *was* eyes to the blind,
> And I *was* feet to the lame.
> I *was* a father to the poor . . .
> I broke the fangs of the wicked,
> And plucked the victim from his teeth' (29:11–13, 15–16, 17).

We are further told that Job's outward lot was as happy as
his character was exemplary. God's blessing was in the most
marked manner bestowed upon his faithful servant, bringing
him the most distinguished prosperity. He was happy in his
family, having seven sons and three daughters, who were all
settled near each other, and near their paternal home, and
lived in the most delightful harmony and fraternal
intercourse. He had large possessions: his wealth in flocks and
herds is recorded, and it is added that he was the greatest of
all the men of the East. And he was treated with the utmost

deference and respect by all classes, and held in the highest
esteem. He says in his retrospect of these happy days:

> When I went out to the gate by the city,
> *When* I took my seat in the open square,
> The young men saw me and hid,
> And the aged arose *and* stood;
> The princes refrained from talking,
> And put *their* hand on their mouth;
> the voice of nobles was hushed,
> and their tongue stuck to the roof of their mouth . . .
> I chose the way for them, and sat as chief;
> So I dwelt as a king in the army (29:7, 25).

There seemed to be nothing to be desired in the way of
worldly prosperity or earthly joy, beyond what he possessed.

Our thoughts are turned so frequently to the discipline of
affliction and the spiritual profit which arises out of it, that
we are in some danger, perhaps, of losing sight of the rule in
the prominence which is given to the exception. And yet
religion has its temporal as well as its eternal rewards.

The blessing of God attends the good, even in this present
life and in regard to their worldly estate. There are promises
of long life and prosperity, as far as it shall serve for God's
glory, and their own good, to all those that keep his
commandments.

> Blessed *is* every one who fears the LORD,
> Who walks in his ways.
> When you eat the labor of your hands,
> You *shall* be happy, and *it shall be* well with you
> (*Psa.* 128:1–2).

> For evildoers shall be cut off;
> But those who wait on the LORD,
> They shall inherit the earth (*Psa.* 37:9).

> Surely *there is* a reward for the righteous;
> Surely He is God who judges in the earth (*Psa* 58:11).

It is true that worldly possessions bring a snare. And our
Saviour said that it is a hard thing for them that have riches

[13]

to enter into the kingdom of God. And an apostle adds, '... not many wise according to the flesh, not many mighty, not many noble, are called' (*1 Cor.* 1:26). So likewise another apostle: 'Has God not chosen the poor of this world to be rich in faith and heirs of the kingdom which he promised to those who love him?' (*James* 2:5).

There is a peril, no doubt, in having a large share of this world's good. The danger is of cleaving to the world unduly, and of setting the affections upon earthly comforts and earthly pleasures – of being content with an earthly portion and ceasing to strive after or long for one that is heavenly. If the heart is given to the world, and worldly objects, be they what they may, become our end and aim, then we are worldly-minded and are not the servants of God. 'If anyone loves the world, the love of the Father is not in him' (*1 John* 2:15). 'You cannot serve God and mammon' (*Matt.* 6:24). They that will be rich, that is, that seek riches as their chief good, and make this their main, controlling object of pursuit, fall into temptation and a snare, and into many foolish and hurtful lusts, which drown men in destruction and perdition. 'For the love of money is a root of all kinds of evil' (*1 Tim.* 6:10). Our Saviour's rule is, 'Seek first the kingdom of God and his righteousness' – first in order of time, first in importance, first in the urgency of desire and in the strenuousness of endeavour – 'and all these things shall be added to you' (*Matt.* 6:33).

If this true order is preserved, then other things may be safely added, and no harm will result. The damage arises from the prevailing disposition to invert this order, to seek the world first, and then as much of heaven as can be had without too great a sacrifice of worldly interests. Now upon the basis both of scriptural teaching and of the common experience of men, it may confidently be affirmed that the true way to a happy life, even in this world, is found in the service of God. Our Saviour announced the universal law when he said, 'For whoever desires to save his life will lose it, but whoever loses his life for My sake will save it' (*Luke* 9:24).

This is a seeming paradox, but it is perpetually verified. He who aims at worldly good fails to attain it. He either is unable to acquire that form of worldly good which he seeks, or, if he gets possession of it, he does not find it what he expected: it proves to be empty and insubstantial, and does not yield the satisfaction which he anticipated and desired. But he who abandons this world as his object, and aims at God's glory instead, gains that and this world too.

It is as in the case of Solomon, who prayed not for riches, nor for long life, but for wisdom. God gave him that he asked: he gave him wisdom, and added long life and riches besides. Selfishness defeats itself: in grasping with desperate eagerness after earthly good, it snatches a painted bubble, which bursts in its hands. Our truest welfare and highest happiness, even if we limit our view to the present life, will be most effectually secured by faithfully serving God and doing his will.

It has passed into a proverb that honesty is the best policy. In a like sense and with similar limitations it is equally true that piety is the best policy. He who refuses to defraud his neighbour, not from any principle of integrity, but simply because he will thus in the end enhance his gains, does not deserve the praise of real honesty. And he who adopts the guise of piety to further worldly ends forfeits alike the approbation of God and the esteem of men. Nevertheless goodness has its temporal rewards.

> Length of days is in [Wisdom's] right hand,
> In her left hand riches and honour' (*Prov.* 3:16).

That this is so is obvious enough, both in general and in its application to communities and masses of men.

Religion fosters those qualities and habits which tend to worldly prosperity and success and to the promotion of the general good. It encourages industry, thrift, and frugality, and thus lends its aid to accumulation, while on the other hand it represses all those forms of vicious indulgence which lead to profligacy, neglect of proper occupation, and wasteful dissipation. A large part of the extreme poverty and suffering that is found in the world is either directly or indirectly the consequence of criminal or wicked conduct, its natural and inevitable retribution affecting the wicked themselves or those connected with them.

And it is not the evils of degraded poverty alone that arise in this way, but miseries that affect wealthier classes, desolating families in high life, withering every joy, and blighting all their possessions. God has set the mark of his disapprobation upon sin by these moral consequences which he has fixed in the world and by which a penalty has been fastened to transgression. These consequences can only be averted by drying up the sources of the evil; and this religion does.

Another fertile cause of suffering and sorrow in the world, which the prevalence of true religion would obliterate, is the injustice and unkindness of man to his fellow-man. The strong oppress the weak, and they who cannot defend themselves are mercilessly trodden in the dust. Each man becomes the antagonist of his fellow, with rival interests, profiting by his downfall; instead of his brother, co-operating with him, mutually helpful and serviceable to each other.

Hence the struggle of injurious competition, none caring in his greed for self-advancement that his neighbour is driven to the wall. Hence those feuds of mutually dependent classes; labour and capital seeking each its own advantage, and forcing hard terms upon the other, or coming to open rupture to the injury of both. Hence discords, tumults, wars, with all the sorrows they occasion and the miseries they entail.

How would the world blossom like an Eden, if religion held full sway, and its golden rule were enshrined in every heart and acted out in every life! And religion is the only salt which can preserve from national corruption and decay. The history of the past utters its warning voice, showing how the downfall of nations swiftly follows on the heels of national prosperity, and the seeds of dissolution are involved in the very materials of their greatness and splendour.

Accumulation multiplies the opportunity and the facilities of indulgence, and public virtue gives way, amid the glittering prizes held out for its allurement.

Recent events have suggested gloomy thoughts to many reflecting minds amongst ourselves. Can virtue and integrity be maintained in our rulers and among our people, amidst the manifold temptations which are now assailing them, and before which, many once trusted and confided in have sadly fallen? If honesty and integrity fail us in the centres of authority, if the enactment and administration of law can be tampered with by corrupting influences, and the public conscience becomes itself debauched by the corruption that is coming in like a flood, what must every sane mind anticipate as the inevitable result?

In this growing – we fear it must be said rapid – decay of virtue and integrity in legislative halls, in some quarters even in courts of justice, and in leading financial circles, the most portentous evils are opening before us. Can they be arrested? The answer to this question depends upon another. Have we vital Christianity enough among us to check the progress of moral decay? Is there that fear of God and love of truth and right among our countrymen, which will insist on honesty and integrity in the administration of public affairs and in the conduct of financial corporations and commercial enterprises?

The religion of the gospel is the stronghold of our national safety and of the perpetuity of our institutions. The more thoroughly this gospel shall leaven our people, the stronger we shall be, the firmer will be the pillars of our national prosperity, and the more abundant and widely diffused will be the blessings enjoyed by all our population.

But the temporal blessedness springing from true religion has its application to individuals as well as to communities and masses. Communities are made up of individuals, and what tends to promote the welfare of the whole must in the same ratio be conducive to the good of its constituent members. Upon this there is no need to dwell; but there are other considerations, which should likewise be taken into the account.

Happiness is not so dependent on external circumstances as many suppose. It is far more powerfully affected by men's own character and disposition. It lies not so much in the abundance of outward sources of enjoyment as in the capacity to enjoy. It is not graduated by wealth, or social position, or success in worldly schemes. They who look at the bare outside of things are often grievously mistaken in their judgements. A splendid mansion may be the home of misery and care. And he who reclines on the most luxurious couch may be a stranger to repose.

When we speak of the blessing of God accompanying fidelity to his service, we do not mean that the pious man will always be rich, or that he will always attain distinction, or that he will be invariably successful in his worldly schemes. But we say that while in ordinary cases he will not be damaged, but rather furthered, even in outward prosperity, by his religion, his real substantial happiness will be vastly promoted. He will the better enjoy what he does possess, he will draw a livelier and purer satisfaction from it, than he would if he had not the love of God in his heart and the fear of God before his eyes.

If his religion has simply taught him this one lesson, in whatsoever state he is, therewith to be content, it has done much to establish and confirm his earthly happiness. For 'godliness with contentment is great gain' (*1 Tim.* 6:6). It frees him from the dominion of evil passions, envy, jealousy, hatred, and the like, which are a fruitful source of discontent. It relieves him from the galling slavery of those in haste to be rich, with its attendant cares, anxieties, and consuming toil. It leads him to see in his earthly lot the appointment of his heavenly Father, and thus cures him of all restless endeavours to overleap bounds he cannot pass. It gives him the consciousness of being at peace with his Maker and with all the world. He has the joy which flows from doing right; and every outgoing of unselfish love, every exercise of pure affection, every act of generous kindness to the needy to which his religion prompts him, is a new source of pleasure.

And all this is additional to the delight of communion with God, the actings of his regenerated faculties, the enjoyment which is inseparably linked with the Christian's duties and privileges and his glorious hopes – in fine, all that is summed up in that significant phrase, 'the joy of the Holy Spirit' (*1 Thess.* 1:6), a joy which is oftentimes inexpressible and full of glory (*1 Pet.* 1:8).

If any man on earth should be a happy man, it is he who is truly religious. Looking barely at this present life, and at the sources of gratification which are opened before us here, the good man is most truly blessed. Religion does not foster gloom: it is the perennial spring of cheerfulness and joy. It does not abridge the enjoyments of life: it multiplies and heightens them. And there is no step that any person can take, more fraught with blessing to himself in this world as well as in the next, than that in which he makes choice of God as his portion and his friend, and pledges himself to be his ever-faithful servant.

3

Satan

Again there was a day when the sons of God came to present themselves before the LORD, and Satan came also among them to present himself before the LORD (Job 2:1).

We are now introduced to a scene in the invisible world of a most impressive and surprising character. The singular spectacle is presented of the Prince of Darkness appearing in the courts of the Most High. He comes not hypocritically in the guise of an angel of light, but in his proper character, with the rest of God's servants, to offer his homage, to receive his commissions, to render his stated account of work done and service performed.

This astonishing and unusual representation has led some to entertain the opinion that the Satan of the book of Job is a different being from the Satan of the later Scriptures. Else how could he have his place among the sons of God? How could he come with them at stated times to present himself before the LORD? How could this be said of the enemy of God and the adversary of all goodness? A deeper view of this passage, however, reveals the harmony between the character in which Satan appears here and that which he maintains throughout the rest of the Word of God. He is not a mere spy, traversing the earth and intent upon ferreting out all that he can discover. He is the old spirit of malice and wickedness, aiming to pervert men from the right ways of the LORD, and to destroy all goodness as far as it is in his power.

And there is a profound meaning in his appearing here among the sons of God before the LORD. It is designed to express his subordination and subjection to divine control. He cannot act untrammelled and at his own discretion. He is not at liberty to pursue his mischievous designs to whatever extent he may choose. There is a superior restraint to which he is obliged to bow, a superior will that sets limits to his rage, and allows him even within these limits to act out his evil nature only for the sake of some divine end, which he is made to be instrumental in achieving.[1] It is evil in the person of its arch-representative and head, subject to good and constrained to be its minister. It is Satan actually exhibited in the attitude of a servant of God, and made subservient to the discipline and training of his people.

Satan is the enemy of goodness and the enemy of man. With the powers of an archangel, and with the malice and subtlety of a fiend, he is intent on our destruction, and hesitates at nothing by which it can be accomplished. He pursues his mischievous designs with sleepless vigilance and untiring assiduity. Invisible to human eyes, he has all the advantage of secrecy, and taking his victims at unawares. He has his tools and associates in vast numbers of spirits of wickedness, who acknowledge him as their head, and are animated with a rage and cunning similar to his own; and in wicked men who are led captive by him at his will; and even in friendly hands from whom no danger is suspected, and who little think whose commission they are unwittingly

---

[1] The singular passage 1 Kings 22:19–22 affords a remarkable parallel, whose figurative dress may perhaps have been suggested by the symbolical language here employed.

fulfilling. He has a control over external nature and over the bodies of men, which we have no means of estimating, but which can only be conjectured from such facts as the disasters he brought upon Job, and the maladies he caused in the time of our Lord. And, more than all, he has direct access to our souls: he can touch in some incomprehensible way the springs of feeling and conduct, and exert an influence over us, which it may well make us shudder to think of.

All this is terrible. It is a dreadful thing to have a constant consciousness of danger, and especially of unknown danger; to apprehend that an implacable and unscrupulous foe is seeking your life, and that he has woven his plot so stealthily that you know not when you are safe, nor whom to trust. But the assassin can only kill the body. Satan is a murderer of souls. It is an awful thing to be exposed to his treacherous solicitations. To come under his power is perdition. It is to be alienated from God and to incur the sentence of everlasting death. To yield to him in ever so slight a degree is to contract untold guilt, to bring ourselves under the displeasure of God, and put our eternal all in jeopardy. And yet we have no might to stand up against him. Surely, if there is any petition that we offer in all sincerity and with agonizing fervency, that which our blessed Lord has taught us should be so offered,

And do not lead us into temptation,
But deliver us from the evil one (*Matt.* 6:13).

And yet these temptations cannot be escaped. It may be said, in a sense which is in no danger of being misunderstood, that by an ordinance of God they belong to this present state. Jesus was tempted of the devil; and the disciple is not above his Lord. The members must be made like their head. 'We must through many tribulations enter the kingdom of God' (*Acts* 14:22). Fightings and fears beset the passage to the crown. The peril is awful, but success is glorious. 'Blessed *is* the man who endures temptation; for when he has been approved, he will receive the crown of life' (*James* 1:12).

Before entering strictly upon the development of the teachings of this book, which is the chief design of this little treatise, we will devote a chapter to a preliminary inquiry of no small practical importance. What is the design of God in subjecting his people to this terrible ordeal? What are the disciplinary ends of the temptations of Satan, and how may we best attain them?

And to this we answer:—

1. They should drive us to take refuge in God. One grand aim of the earthly discipline of God's people, in all its parts, is to bring them to a closer acquaintance with him and dependence upon him. They are made to learn more and more of his fulness, and to draw from him larger and richer supplies. All the disclosures of his grace and of his unbounded resources made in his Word are designed to bring them to himself as to an overflowing fountain, that they may drink the water of life freely. But in order that they may be stimulated to avail themselves of these benefits, and not perish in sight of abundance, an inward appetite is necessary, a hungering and thirsting after God, a craving for those blessings which he has to bestow. And the more imperative and urgent the sense of need which is awakened, the louder will be the cry for help, and the more importunate the application for it.

Here precisely the temptations of the Evil One have their place in God's great scheme of training. Every instinct of self-preservation in a gracious soul should lead it to cry mightily unto God for his delivering aid. Every temptation is attended with an imminence of peril, which should startle us out of our security, and lead us to fly for safety to him who alone can save.

He who has any just sense of his own weakness and frailty, and of the frightful evil of sin, must be incessant in his entreaties that he may be upheld in steadfastness by an almighty arm, and guarded from the assaults of one who succeeded even in enticing angels to their fall, and prevailed over our first parents in all the vigour of their early integrity, and to whom we shall prove an easy prey, unless One, stronger than the strong man armed, interferes for our rescue.

A proper sense of our peril will not only tend to beget the general conviction that in God alone is our help, but will, in addition, lead us to fasten upon those particular assurances and grounds of encouragement which are afforded by him for just such a crisis as this. The knowledge of the vast power of our spiritual adversary will lead us to take refuge in the omnipotence of God, to place a new value upon this glorious attribute, to avail ourselves of it as a basis of repose and confidence, to experience in our daily consciousness what it is to have a God of such infinite resources to supply our pressing need.

The almighty power of God is then no longer an abstraction to us – an intellectual conviction – but a present practical necessity; not a perfection which we distantly contemplate, but one by which we live and without which we perish. The dire necessity which drives us to the fount of life is, in its results, an incalculable blessing. And the temptation of Satan, which terrifies the soul out of all self-dependence and creature-dependence, and compels it to find refuge in an almighty Saviour, has accomplished a gracious end.

And as with this, so with other perfections of the ever-blessed God, and with the precious promises of his Word, and with the merciful provisions of the covenant of grace, and with the priceless salvation of our Lord Jesus Christ. The tempted soul learns afresh how to prize them, and embrace them, and cling to them, and rest upon them, and live by them.

To what can he have recourse for protection against the subtlety and craft of Satan but the infinite wisdom and knowledge of God? How his dread of the rage of Satan enhances to him the value of the love of God! His unseen approaches exalt in our esteem, God's gracious omnipresence. His access to our minds and hearts can only be baffled or rendered abortive by the indwelling and illumination of the Holy Ghost. What new delight is awakened by the thought of God's providential control, when we remember that he who has set the seas their bound restrains likewise the malice of Satan, suffers him not to overstep the limits which our Father's love has fixed, and will not allow his people to be tempted above that they are able to bear, or without providing a way of escape for them that they be not overcome thereby! And what completeness is imparted to Christ's redemption, when we see that he triumphed over Satan, bruised the serpent in the dust, and shall bruise him under his people's feet! With what new eagerness will these dreaded temptations compel us to look to the cross, which is the symbol and pledge of victory over the destroyer!

2. The temptations of Satan answer the important purpose of training the believer in the duties and exercises of the Christian warfare. The sacred historian informs us that there was a providential design in leaving a remnant of the Canaanites in the land of Israel, namely to teach the skills of war to succeeding generations of the people. There is no teacher like necessity, and no training in the military art comparable to that enforced by actual hostilities.

What emphasis there is in that direction of the apostle, 'Put on the whole armour of God, that you may be able to stand against the wiles of the devil'! (*Eph.* 6:11) It is not a time of peace and security, but of deadly conflict. It will not do to remain defenceless, and no armour that is defective or incomplete will answer in this terrible exigency. The weapons of our adversary will be swift to find it, if there be one weak or unguarded spot from head to foot. And what a school for practice in all the measures of offence and defence is this contest for life or death with such a foe! It is said of a great master in the art of war, that he learned his skill in strategy entirely from the powerful and able leaders with whom he was obliged to cope. The Christian, in his protracted and stubborn contest with the wiliest of all antagonists, cannot fail to make distinguished progress in spiritual generalship, as well as to develop the qualities of a good soldier of Jesus Christ.

Nothing is better adapted to call forth a manly vigour than the necessity of strenuous exertion. The struggles one must make, the endeavours one must put forth to resist temptation and to overcome the evil one, react to the greatest advantage upon Christian character. The circumspection necessary to escape his insidious designs, the vigilance of one who is obliged to be ever on his guard, the fixed determination of one who has set his face like a flint for the celestial city, and who has resolved that he will be true to his God and his Saviour at all hazards, tend to elevate rapidly the standard of the inner life.

And these temptations exhibit grace as well as develop it. It can never be shown either to himself or to others what a man is until he is tried. The constancy of Job and the power of his faith could never have been made to appear so conspicuous, if it had not been for the severity of the test to which he was subjected. This lay not only in the accumulated sorrows by which he was so suddenly overwhelmed, but chiefly in the suggestions of the tempter, who was mercilessly goading him on to give up his confidence in God, and to renounce his service. It was these sore temptations, based on the mystery of dispensations which he could not unravel, and backed by a logic which he knew not how to confute, which tortured him almost to despair, and wrung from him those bitter wailings with which the book abounds. And yet in spite of all, out of the midst of the depths we hear him utter in the very face of the tempter his unabated trust in God, 'I know that my Redeemer lives' (19:25).

3. The temptations of Satan, if properly met, may be made a means of intensifying our hatred of sin. He who has barely escaped the fangs of a venomous reptile will ever after entertain a deeper abhorrence of it. Sin is in every temptation offered to our choice. But it need only be stripped of its disguises to present it in its repulsive and odious features, and make us shrink with loathing from the contact. The very act of repelling it will cultivate a spiritual sensitiveness which can less and less endure its hateful presence.

4. But, in the fourth place, observe that temptation may be an aid to self-knowledge. The germs of evil often lie undeveloped in the heart, and the man himself never suspects their existence until under the influence of some sudden or strong temptation they are brought to light. It is like the searching tests of the assayer exposing the presence of alloy in what might easily have passed for sterling metal. Such mortification enters into the Christian's daily experience by way of humiliating discoveries of the strength of latent corruption and unsubdued propensities to evil, appetites which he supposed he had under subjection, resuming the mastery in some fatal moment; the feebleness of his resolutions, insincerity in motives, imperfection in his best services.

If these discoveries serve to humble him in the dust, and bring him in penitent brokenness of heart to sue for pardoning mercy, and lead him to be more watchful against his besetting sins, the ends of divine grace in suffering him to be overtaken by this temptation will be answered.

It was thus with Job. God himself testified that there was none like him on the earth, a blameless and upright man, one who feared God and shunned evil (1:8). And yet there was a leaven of corruption in his imperfectly sanctified nature, of which he was not aware, until by the terrible thrusts of Satan it was exposed. Underneath his really sincere and fervent piety there was a taint of self-righteousness, which made him smart as he did under the reproaches of his friends, and which, in the awful darkness of that mysterious dispensation in which he was enshrouded, led him even to the length of justifying himself rather than God.

Brought at last to himself, and dismayed at the thought of what he had allowed himself to utter, he says, 'I abhor *myself*, and repent in dust and ashes' (42:6). The design of God in this severe but salutary discipline was accomplished. Job had been led to know himself better than he did before, and he was humbled by this knowledge. The evil which before lurked within him unsuspected, was detected and renounced.

5. The temptations of Satan afford the opportunity for grace to develop itself in forms which otherwise it could not assume. Thus all that is implied in patient continuance in well-doing could have no place under other circumstances than those in which we are. The blessed inhabitants of that upper sphere, where sin and sorrow never enter, know not what it is to drag for ever after them this body of corruption, to be checked and hampered in all their aspirations by a law of sin in their members, to maintain their steadfastness amid surrounding foes, to preserve the flame of piety bright and clear under the deadening influences of this ungodly world, to keep a cheerful hope in the midst of discouragement and ill success, and doubts and fears; or to continue to trust unwaveringly in the Lord, when deprived of the light of his countenance.

Although God may be glorified and his law honoured by the unhesitating obedience rendered by the countless ranks of those who do not understand from their own experience what temptation means, it would appear as though there was something yet more signal and illustrious in that willing obedience which costs many a weary effort and many a painful struggle in that loyalty to Jesus which is maintained, not amidst the sympathy and applause of those who likewise adore his name, but in the face of derision, obloquy, and persecution; in that unfaltering submission, which can say not merely in the sunlight of the throne, but in the howlings of the pitiless tempest, 'Your will be done' (*Matt.* 26:42). The post of danger is the post of honour, if it be well and bravely defended. Is it no honour, then, which the LORD of all puts upon faithful souls when he sets them in the fore-front of the battle, where the fiery darts of the adversary shower thickly around them, and bids them stand firmly there, and bravely maintain his cause? Might not angels envy them this exalted privilege?

And then, besides, there are forms of pious service which are conditioned by the temptations of Satan, directed not upon the actors themselves, but upon others – those holy

Christlike ministrations to the sinful and the suffering, the ignorant and the needy – those beautiful acts of heaven-born charity which so illustrate and adorn the gospel, and shed a fragrance so pleasing both to God and man – all this belongs to a world where sin abounds, and Satan has free scope, and can appear nowhere else.

6. A sixth gracious end, which temptations may be designed to accomplish, is to wean the heart from the love of this present world. It is sheer cowardice or faint-heartedness in a soldier to be for ever whining about the dangers or hardships of the campaign, and importuning for a release. And it would be reprehensible in the Christian to be indolently sighing for the coming rest, merely to escape the toil of labouring in his Master's service.

But this error is far less common than the opposite extreme of clinging unduly to this vain world, and having the affections too firmly rooted here. To counteract this dangerous tendency, measures must be employed to loosen this attachment, by making the world seem less desirable, and causing us to sigh for what is purer and better. The weariness induced by the incessant conflict between the flesh and the spirit often weighs heavily upon the soul. It is a hard thing to be for ever crucifying our corrupt nature, to be always struggling against a power which we find it impossible to subdue, endeavouring to keep down principles and propensities which we strive in vain to eradicate or extinguish, and never able with safety to relax our vigilance or to desist from effort.

And it is disheartening to find how slow is our progress towards the completed conquest, even if we advance at all; how often the ground which we seemed to have won is wrested from us, and foes that we thought slain rise again to their feet as powerful as before. All this, though it should not lead us to abandon the fight while the enemy is still in the field, would make the news of victory more welcome. It gives sweetness to the thought of a world where there shall be no more sin, and into which temptation cannot enter, where inbred lusts and native corruption shall be removed for ever, and Satan shall at length have ceased to annoy. And this suggests the farther thought:–

7. That the future glory shall be heightened by the temptations of this present time, which have been bravely met and successfully resisted. It is not merely that the coming blessedness shall be an ample compensation for all that tempted souls can now endure, that the flood of joy shall swallow up all thought of present pains, and 'the light affliction, which is for a moment, shall be followed by a far more exceeding and eternal weight of glory' (*2 Cor.* 4:17). But this glory shall, in various ways, be directly enhanced by those temptations, in so far as they have not been criminally yielded to, but in the name of the Master stoutly repelled. And thus what Satan intended for your hurt shall be converted into a source of everlasting profit. The experience of rest shall be heightened by the contrast of the antecedent toil and strife; and the felicity granted to the ransomed soul shall be likewise enhanced in its absolute amount.

If the reward, though wholly the gift of grace, is in proportion to the service done or the fidelity shown, duty resolutely performed in the face of temptations of the evil one will surely receive a marked and signal acknowledgement. The training given to the spiritual faculties in the exercises of the Christian warfare, the development and expansion thence resulting to the powers of the soul, bear directly on our capacity for bliss and holiness. They who have attained the highest measure of fitness thus for the enjoyments of heaven shall have the largest experience of its blessedness. And, further, those who have been driven by the assaults of the adversary into the closest union with their covenant God, and the most entire dependence upon him, shall for this reason again partake most freely of those joys which flow from endless communion with the infinite source of all blessedness.

8. And lastly, the temptations of Satan redound to the glory of divine grace. It belongs to the magnificence of God's universal government that opposition and hostility, to whatever degree and from whatever quarter, instead of tending to

thwart or retard his plans, invariably contribute to further and promote them. Satan forms no exception. This arch-fiend, with all his legions and the entire kingdom of evil which he instigates and controls, in spite of their gathered forces and formidable numbers, and subtle craft and hellish spite, is absolutely powerless to prevent or to retard the execution of the least of God's designs. An infant in the arms is not more impotent to arrest the movement of the spheres than Satan is to check the fulfilment of God's sovereign decrees.

And this absolute control is rendered more illustrious by the manner of its exercise. It is not by bringing the resources of omnipotence to overpower the devil and his crew, and to chain them in the awful prison-house prepared for them, so that, driven entirely away from the theatre of his operations, they can no longer interfere with or obstruct them. On the contrary, Satan is allowed free range, as the prince of the power of the air. He has installed himself as the god of this world. He is busy with his plans and his combinations. They are laid with consummate skill, and he is working them with tremendous energy. He is labouring to undo the work of God, to defeat the atonement, to destroy souls whom Christ would save.

But his machinations shall recoil upon himself. Do what he may, let him rage as he please, let him accomplish his worst, and he is after all only building up what in his blind fury and malice he is endeavouring to tear down. The decrees which he would frustrate embrace himself and all his hateful deeds, as agencies co-operating to their fulfilment. With all his hatred of God and spite against his people, he cannot emancipate himself from that sovereign control, which binds him to God's service. In all his blasphemous designs he is, in spite of himself, doing the work of God. In his rebellious efforts to dethrone the Most High, he is actually paying him submissive homage. In moving heaven and earth to accomplish the perdition of those whom Christ has ransomed, he is actually fitting them for glory. Fiend as he is, full of bitterness and malignity, and intent on every form of mischief, he is constrained to be that which he most abhors, and is furthest from his intentions and desires, helpful and auxiliary to the designs of grace. Like the sons of God who assemble in the presence of the Infinite Majesty to receive the commissions of the King of kings, prompt to do his bidding and to execute his will, Satan is, though most reluctantly, and in a different sense from them, yet as really and as truly, in the case of those who, like Job, steadfastly resist his insidious assaults, a ministering spirit sent forth to minister to them who shall be heirs of salvation.

But the enforced subordination of this spirit of malice and wickedness to the ends of divine mercy and grace is rendered yet more illustrious, both to the praise of God's glory and to Satan's everlasting shame and crushing defeat by another particular in the achievement of this triumph. This is the immediate agency by which his subjugation is effected.

The New Testament seer beheld a vision of war in heaven. 'Michael and his angels fought with the dragon; and the dragon and his angels fought, but they did not prevail, nor was a place found for them in heaven any longer. So the great dragon was cast out, that serpent of old, called the Devil and Satan, who deceives the whole world; he was cast to the earth, and his angels were cast out with him' (*Rev.* 12:7–9). Here, though he was defeated, it was by an antagonist worthy to cope with him. The rival forces fairly matched his own; and, however disastrous his overthrow, there was no dishonour in falling by such hands.

But when, smarting under his defeat in heaven, he went to make war with them which keep the commandments of God, and have the testimony of Jesus Christ, he prepared for himself a most ignominious repulse. He who aspired to be the leader of the host of heaven, and drew a third part of the angels in his fall, assaults the feeble children of men, and utterly fails to compass the ruin of one of them upon whom Jesus has set his love. He can terrify them; he can torture them; he can make them drag on the weary conflict with sin and corruption while life lasts; he can extort from them bitter groans of agonizing distress; he can shower upon them his fiery darts; but he cannot destroy them. The glimmering spark, which divine grace has kindled, he cannot with all the floods of temptation extinguish. Satan cannot by any means harm the feeblest of God's saints, who stands up against him in the name of the Lord. If he have on the armour with which divine grace has furnished him, and use aright the weapons with which he is supplied, and in humble dependence on his Lord abides faithful at his post, he is invincible; and the boastful foe, who came upon him ready to swallow him up, shall be driven back in shame and confusion. Resist the devil, and he will flee from you.

In the rapid view which has been taken of this subject, our attention has been confined to the temptations of Satan, as directed against the individual believer. Our limits will not allow us to extend our view to his assaults upon the kingdom of God in its collective capacity, and see how there, too, he most unwittingly acts under orders from the throne; how, in stirring up opposers to combat the truth of God, he but contributes to clear its statements, to unfold its richness, and render its defences more impregnable; how all his designs upon the Church, whether in provoking against her the hostility of the world, sowing dissensions in her own ranks, or in whatever way he may endeavour her injury, are unable to effect her overthrow.

The gates of hell cannot prevail against the Church. The earthquake, which in its violent upheaval threatens to demolish the city of God, but shows how absolutely secure its firm foundations are. He may shake earth and heaven, and the crash will only bring down what he had himself essayed to build with rude untempered mortar, and it will only reveal in its unique stability, and bring to view in its fair proportions, free from every disfiguring addition, the solid, immovable building of God.

And now in this warfare we are engaged. The temptations of Satan are not to be escaped: no sheltered position, no seclusion from the world, no sacredness of occupation, can screen us from them. The only question is, Shall they prove our infinite damage, or shall they be made to recoil harmless and pointless? It is the most awful question which we can be summoned to answer; and yet the decision of this question may be said to have been placed by the infinite grace of God within our own control. If you yield to the tempter, you become his helpless prey. If you steadfastly resist him, confiding in the grace of God and the salvation of Jesus, he cannot touch a hair of your head. Temptation and sin, if you bravely resist them, will react to your everlasting welfare: your position is impregnable, the protection is ample, the armament is invincible, the supplies abundant, and the fortress can never be entered by the enemy, unless betrayed into his power by your own treacherous hands.

4

Job in Affliction

The LORD gave, and the LORD has taken away; blessed be the name of the LORD (Job 1:21).
Shall we indeed accept good from God, and shall we not accept adversity? (Job 2:10).

We have seen Job in his piety and prosperous estate. We are now to see him in his sad reverses, and to witness his behaviour in affliction. A change of circumstances often makes a great change in men themselves, or at least exposes a new and previously unsuspected side of their character, and develops unlooked-for results. Sometimes it brings to light defects that had never been dreamed of in those who were esteemed almost faultless; sometimes it reveals unanticipated excellencies. Emergencies are the making of some men, and the destruction of others. The former rise in greatness, and in every noble quality of soul, in proportion to the increasing demands of the occasion. The latter are unable to abide the severity of the test applied to them, and fall before it. How will it be with Job?

A disclosure is made at the outset, to the readers of this book, of things that are concealed from the human actors in it. The veil that hides the unseen world is partially drawn aside, so as to afford us a glimpse of a spiritual agent, who is to give a new turn to events. The arch-enemy of man has had his eye upon Job. True to the instincts of his own vile nature, he has no faith in the reality of goodness. He sees in the piety of Job nothing but a refined form of selfishness. He serves God because it is his interest to do so. God protects and blesses him, and as a matter of course he inclines to the quarter from which the favours come; but if these favours were to cease, the tempter urges, Job's piety would vanish with them. His goodness has its spring in its attendant rewards: withhold the latter, and Job will soon take leave of God and his service, which no longer yields him any advantage.

Satan is allowed to bring to an issue this question which he has raised. He may put Job's piety to the test, and in him he may test the question whether there is such a thing as real piety in the earth, a piety that is not merely self-seeking and actuated by a hope of gain, but which heartily loves the right and cleaves to it, and chooses the service of God though no hope of profit can attach to so doing.

Job is on trial, though he knows it not; and unfriendly eyes are eagerly watching for his halting. And he is on trial not merely for himself: the cause of religion is represented in him, the cause of God on earth, though he is also unconscious of the dignity of his position and of the sacredness of the interest which he is set to sustain, and of the fact that the eyes of the Lord of all are turned upon him with approval, and with a lively concern for the favourable issue of the struggle in which he is engaged.

Of the spiritual significance of this transaction, Job is profoundly ignorant. He feels the terrible pressure of his heavy sorrows, but he is not aware that they have been sent upon him as a test of character. He knows nothing of Satan's malicious designs, who seeks to prove his piety a pretence.

He knows nothing of the sovereign purpose of God, who means to establish its reality and power to the confusion of the tempter.

It is with trembling apprehension that we see such power granted to this unseen adversary, with liberty to use it against the unsuspecting patriarch: 'Behold, all that he has *is* in your power' (1:12). 'Behold, he *is* in your hand' (2:6). The contest seems fearfully unequal between this arch-fiend and mortal man, however firm his integrity, whatever the sincerity and strength of his piety. It reassures us somewhat, however, when we observe that the tempter is, after all, limited and restrained by Job's almighty guardian and friend. The fiend cannot frame and carry out his malevolent designs unchecked. He acts only by sufferance. He must have leave from the Most High, before he can touch Job at all to harm him or lay his hand upon any thing that he has. And, when permission is given, it is within fixed limits, which he may not overstep.

When Job's property was put at Satan's disposal, it was with the accompanying restriction: 'Only do not lay a hand on his *person*' (1:12). When Job's own person was further subjected to his power, it was with the added requirement, 'But spare his life' (2:6). With all the limitations, however, a tremendous range was conceded to this enemy of all right-eousness, and the assault which he makes is a frightful one. Can Job endure the shock?

In order that we may properly appreciate the conduct of Job in his affliction, we must further take into account another consideration. Job went into his trial destitute of many of those firm supports and grounds of consolation which are now so plentifully supplied to suffering saints. Those revelations had not yet been made upon which the believer now so firmly rests his hope in times of deep distress. Truths, which are as familiar to us as household words in the gracious disclosures of the gospel, had never yet been clearly set before the minds of men.

Perhaps it may be said that the faintest conceptions of them had scarcely dawned on any human consciousness. The king's broad highway through the wilderness of earthly sorrow, along which suffering pilgrims can now pass in comparative safety and comfort, had not then been constructed. Its route had not even been surveyed, nor a pathway broken. Job was one of the hardy pioneers to whom this primary task was committed.

He had to make his own way, without guide or chart or knowledge of the ground, through the tangled, trackless, howling waste; with no light to relieve the darkness of the night that enveloped him but the lone pole-star of his unshaken trust in God, and this, alas! dimmed often, and obscured by the black, threatening clouds which swept athwart his sky, though ever and anon peering forth afresh; unsheltered, too, from the tempest and the storm, which broke over him without mercy. Precipices yawned at his feet, swollen streams ran across his route, and there were treacherous bogs in which he might be hopelessly mired. Is it strange if his stout heart quailed at the terrors which surrounded him? Is it strange if groans of distress were extorted from him?

Yet, in spite of all, he pushed his way through, and the path which he opened has defined the route for many travellers since. There is not a weary sufferer in Christendom who is not indebted to the patriarch of Uz, who has not been helped and aided by his example of fortitude and constancy, and in addition had reason to be grateful for the lessons of comfort and hope transmitted to us from him.

He grappled with the mystery of affliction in all its unexplained darkness and difficulty, until his own soul found rest. Those cheering views of truth, to which he fought his way, or which were graciously vouchsafed to him in his trial, have been the heritage of God's people ever since.

Think for a moment what it would be to encounter crushing sorrows not only without Calvary and Gethsemane and the sympathy of the incarnate Son of God, who is himself touched with the feeling of our infirmities, for he was in all points tempted like as we are, yet without sin; but to go into trials that offer no bright spot this side the grave, with no clear views of that eternal blessedness, in comparison with which all earthly sorrows, however grievous in themselves, and long continued, are nevertheless light and momentary; without the assurance that present griefs and sufferings shall be overbalanced and outweighed by that far more exceeding and eternal weight of glory, whose absolute amount they shall themselves greatly enhance.

What would it be to encounter frowning providences without the distinct understanding that these are nevertheless consistent with the abiding, unchanging love of our heavenly Father? They are not tokens of his displeasure; they are not evidences that he has withdrawn his love or has shut up his tender mercies. On the contrary, 'whom the LORD loves he chastens' (*Heb.* 12:6). There is a paternal discipline in affliction. It has a gracious design, and will have a salutary result. The rod is in a loving Father's hand: its strokes are not capriciously nor unkindly given, they are administered solely for our good.

Deprive the sufferer of the solace afforded by his knowledge of these precious truths, hide from him the benefit to be derived from affliction, take away his consciousness of the divine love in the midst of it all, and remove from him the assurance of the everlasting reward which shall infinitely more than compensate all that he now endures, and how defenceless would he appear in the presence of heavy griefs! These wellsprings of consolation had not yet been opened. These comforting truths had never found utterance in human speech. Simple and obvious as they now appear to us from frequent repetition, and belonging to the very alphabet of our religion, they had never been distinctly formulated, and no clear conception of them had ever been reached.

Job must fight the battle without the aids which his experience as well as later revelations have furnished us. His sorrows came upon him, not for his own sake merely, but for ours. A new lesson was to be given to the world; and Job was to be the medium of instruction. The stream of adversity swells around him, until in danger of sinking he is compelled to struggle with all his might to get upon the sure foundation. Where he finds firm footing, other children of sorrow may safely tread.

The spectacle before us, then, is that of this eminent man of God, chosen to be the leader of the band of sufferers in their mortal conflict with evil and the evil one. He goes into the strife unpractised and unawares. The onset of the foe is fierce and furious. Will even Job be able to stand in the evil day?

The conflict unfolds itself in three successive stages of growing violence, and the demeanour of this holy man is depicted to us in each. In the first, we behold him in one evil day suddenly and irretrievably despoiled of all his possessions. In the morning his sky was without a cloud. He was in the midst of the prosperous abundance which he had long enjoyed, and seemed to have every reason to feel secure of its continuance. It was in fact a day of special festivity and family reunion; and, so far from leading to the anticipation of evil, it was an occasion of more than ordinary joy. Happy in his children, and in his possessions, and in the respect and consideration universally accorded to him, his cup of blessing overflowed. And there was nothing to suggest the likelihood of a coming reverse.

And yet, before that day was ended, everything was gone. To such destitution was he reduced that his condition is aptly likened to that of a new-born child. He came naked into the world; and now that he had been stripped of all, he shall leave it as naked as he came.

Suddenly, and without a moment's warning, the storm of calamity burst over the head of the doomed patriarch. One messenger of evil chased another with tidings of disaster. One had not ended his tale of loss before another came with a tale more doleful still. His oxen and his asses were driven off by the wild and roving tribe of the Sabeans; his sheep were consumed by fire from heaven; his camels were carried away by plundering bands of Chaldeans; and his servants put to the sword. And, to complete the dismal intelligence of woe, the house in which his children were assembled, and passing the hours in glad hilarity, was overturned by a tornado and fell upon them all, crushing them to death. In one moment of terrible reverse the stricken patriarch is bereaved of his children and despoiled of his property. All is taken from him in an instant; and, of all that he had cherished and delighted in and prized of earthly good, he has nothing left.

If the calamity had been less sweeping and universal, it would not have been so overwhelming. If something had been spared him, if it had been only a part of his property and not the whole which was taken, the loss might still have been considerable, it might have been heavy, it might have involved the greater part of his fortune; still, if he had not lost all, it would have been easier to bear it with equanimity.

Or though all his property were taken from him, if those possessions had been left which were dearer far than flocks and herds, those precious domestic treasures which he valued beyond all his wealth – if his beloved children had been spared, it would have been easier to bear the loss of all beside. It would have been hard to part with one of that cherished circle that he prized so much and loved so fondly; but to lose not only one, nor two, nor three, but all, and all at once, this was bereavement and desolation indeed.

If the blows had not fallen so suddenly and in such quick succession; if he could have had some time in which to steady himself for the shock; if there had been some intervals of relief in which he could have summoned all his strength to meet the coming blows, it would have seemed less dreadful, it would not have been so crushing as when the whole dire weight came down upon him at a stroke.

By this accumulation of sorrows so suddenly sprung upon Job, the violence of the attack was increased to the utmost, and thus his steadfastness was put to the severest test. Can the tempter drive him thus to give up his integrity and abandon his trust in God? Under the pressure of sore affliction men are in danger of falling into one or other of two opposite

extremes, either of which is inconsistent with fidelity to the
Lord's service. The first is that of repining and murmuring at
the divine allotment: the other is that of bearing it in a spirit
of stoical indifference. The wise man warns us against both.

My son, do not despise the chastening of the LORD,
Nor be discouraged when you are rebuked by Him
(*Heb.* 12:5).

Job avoided both these dangers in that subdued but noble
demeanour which has been in all ages since the model of
submissive resignation. The stricken patriarch, bowed with
grief, adopts the tokens of the most profound humiliation
and sorrow: he rent his mantle, and shaved his head, and fell
down upon the ground. Not to sit in sullen silence, and
brood despondently over the terrible losses which he had
sustained; not to complain of the providence of God, which
had dealt so hardly with him: No, he prostrates himself in
reverential worship; he bows with meek submission to him
who had smitten him; and his only language is that of grateful adoration to the Source of all blessings, who in removing
all had but taken away what he himself had given. Job fell
down upon the ground and worshipped; and said:

Naked I came from my mother's womb,
And naked shall I return there.
The LORD gave, and the LORD has taken away;
Blessed be the name of the LORD (1:21).

Can humble, trustful piety reach a sublimer utterance than
this? He has been cast down from the height of his prosperity; has suffered the total wreck of his fortune and the loss of
all his family; he is weighed to the earth with his crushing
sorrows; and yet, with bleeding heart and prostrate form, this
venerable man utters not one word of complaint. So far is he
from giving up his confidence in the goodness of the Lord,
that he strengthens himself in this confidence by the very
greatness of the calamity that he has suffered, and draws his
argument of praise for the multitude of God's mercies from
the very bitterness of the cup that is now pressed to his lips.

The submission of Job is not merely that he yields to what is inevitable; that seeing the stroke of fate has fallen, and its blow cannot be turned aside, and the past cannot be undone, he resigns himself to what is beyond the possibility of repair. Nor does he merely succumb to Omnipotence, convinced that it is futile to resist what the almighty God has appointed. None can stay his hand, or prevent the execution of his sovereign will. It can be of no avail to oppose himself to him, and so he subsides, in forced acquiescence. Nor is it merely the rectitude of the infinite Ruler before which he falls prostrate, who has a right to do as he will with his own, and who can dispose of his creatures according to his sovereign pleasure.

Job meekly bows not before the stroke of inevitable fate, not simply before the resistless energy of almighty power, nor simply before the righteous control of the sovereign Ruler; but before the goodness of the Lord, a sense of which now fills his heart proportioned to the magnitude of the reverse which he has sustained. 'The LORD gave, and the LORD has taken away; blessed be the name of the LORD' (1:21). The bitterness of his loss is made the measure of the preciousness of the blessings God had given. The severity of his trial consists in parting with what God had bestowed.

Every pang that now rends his heart is a fresh proof how gracious God has been. The magnitude of the loss determines the value of the gift, and the depth of his anguish enhances his grateful sense of the goodness of the Giver. The more deeply he mourns the treasures which have been taken away from him, the higher is his appreciation of the gracious kindness of him who bestowed them. Thus the more profoundly he grieves, the more fervently he still blesses the name of the Lord,

Not that he sees the goodness of God in afflicting him. This was a lesson Job had not yet learned. The benefits and uses of affliction, and the gracious design with which it is sent of God, had not yet been revealed. It was through these trials of Job himself, and the disclosure of his purposes thus given, and the providential issue of his dealings with his servant, that the first rays of light were shed on this dark and mysterious subject. It was partly in order to afford an occasion for giving these lessons to the world, which might lighten the sorrows, and ease the burdens, and mitigate the trials of subsequent sufferers, that these distresses were sent on Job. Thus did he in a measure suffer for our sakes, and by his stripes we are healed (*Isa.* 53:5); as a forerunner and a type of the great Prince of sufferers, of whom this was true in its strictest and highest sense.

But these lessons, which we have learned from the example of Job and the measures of God's grace with him, as well as from later revelations, were all unknown as yet to the patriarch himself. He knew not that affliction was a means of grace; that there was healing in the bitter draught; that there was mercy in these seeming frowns; that all that he experienced was in fact the chastisement of love. He knew not even that it was a trial and a test of his integrity and pious faith in God; and that the Lord regarded with complacent approbation his steadfast endurance of the test thrust upon him by his great adversary.

And it heightens our conception of Job's sterling piety, and gives us loftier apprehensions of the nobility of his character, and enhances to our view his sublimely meek and submissive demeanour, when we see him confronting the unsolved enigma of this mysterious dispensation, and deducing from it fresh matter for grateful praise. He not merely confesses that he who gave might justly withdraw his own, so that, whatever his losses, his mouth is stopped from making any complaint. But the withdrawal of the gift makes him sensible of its greatness, and, instead of drawing from him the language of repining, compels him to the utterance of praise – 'Blessed be the name of the LORD' (1:21).

The first stage of the trial is ended, and the tempter is foiled. The record is, 'In all this Job did not sin nor charge God with wrong' (1:22).

But the tempter is not yet satisfied, and Job's piety must be put to a yet further proof. He has borne with becoming resignation the loss of all outward possessions, the ruin of his property, the decease of his children; but how if the blow should fall not on what he owns, but upon himself?

Satan accordingly meditates a fresh onset, and leave is given him to aggravate the sorrows of Job already so great by an additional disaster. To the calamities previously sent is now added an infliction upon his own person – a most distressing, offensive, and acute disease, one of the symptoms of which was an eruption of painful ulcers, covering his entire body. He was smitten with sore boils from the sole of his foot to his crown. 'And he took for himself a potsherd with which to scrape himself while he sat in the midst of the ashes' (2:8).

Can Job bear up under this new distress? What will be the effect of pain and bodily suffering added to the shock of former sorrows? Now that he is weakened by disease and distracted by torturing anguish in every member of his body, will it be strange if the trustful submission which he has maintained hitherto gives way? And though he has borne his previous trials with noble fortitude, and he has seen his property swept away, and his children taken from him with tranquil resignation, he should be unable to withstand the pressure of this new calamity, and physical suffering should extort from him murmurs and repining words, and lead him to cherish hard thoughts of God, and give up his trust in his goodness and his gracious providence; and thus the tempter should at length succeed, and Job's piety be put to a test which it could not bear?

The trial proves too much for his wife. Her fortitude forsakes her at this new spectacle of woe. 'Do you still hold fast to your integrity?', she says to him, 'Curse God' – or rather, Take leave of God, abandon his service – 'and die' (2:9). The wife of Job has often been misjudged, and the meaning of her words misunderstood. She has been censured as though she were destitute of piety, had neither love nor sympathy for her husband, and were lacking, in fact, in common humanity. It has even been hinted that Satan showed his hostility to Job no less in sparing her to be a torment to him than in taking the lives of his children. The representation is frequently made, that, never having sympathized with Job in his piety, she was provoked that he should maintain it still when it had proved so unprofitable and was so poorly rewarded.

And she bids him curse God and die, as though she would have him bid defiance to his Maker, from whom he received nothing but unmerited injuries and ill-treatment; as though she would have him upbraid him with the causeless suffering he had brought upon him, if he perished for it; with the intimation perhaps that he might as well die in the wretched condition in which he then was, it would the sooner end his misery; and possibly also with the hard-hearted suggestion that it was of little concern to her, as he had ceased to be any thing but a burden, of which she was willing to be relieved.

We cannot but look upon this severity of censure as quite undeserved. It is unfair to put the worst construction possible upon the language of Job's wife in this case, and then make her conduct on this occasion the index to her whole life. Such a judgement is altogether misleading and gives a perverted view of the incident itself which is here recorded and of the design with which it is introduced. There is no intimation either here, or in the single allusion subsequently made to the wife of Job, 19:17, that there had been any unhappiness in Job's domestic life; that his wife had been uncongenial to him, a thorn in his side, or anything other than the worthy partner of such a husband, his joy and solace, united with him in heart and life, approving and sharing his uprightness and pious trust in God.

Else in the days of his former prosperity his felicity could not have been as pure and untroubled as it is represented to have been; and when his prosperity again returns there is no intimation that she served in any wise to make his happiness incomplete. And, so far as appears, she had borne their first terrible trial with a like spirit of meek and submissive resignation to that of Job himself. She had faced adversity as bravely as he. At least we hear of no murmur from her lips any more than from his on that dreadful day of disaster and sudden reverse, when property and children were all swept remorselessly away, and they were left destitute and alone in remediless desolation. She offered no word of protest then against Job's utterance of pious resignation. So far as appears, her heart went with his. She, too, parted with her wealth and with her children without one repining word.

But when her last earthly prop is breaking, and her only surviving solace is perishing before her eyes, and she sees her husband in such misery and suffering, and sinking into death by so frightful a disease, she is well-nigh frantic in her despair; her fortitude gives way; her trust in God, which she had cherished hitherto, passes under a cloud. She feels that it is a cruel dispensation, and he is cruel who has inflicted it.

She cannot longer give her adoration to a Being who rewards his faithful worshippers thus; who wantonly sends such dire extremity of woe, and has brought such desolation upon her household and her heart. And she cannot bear to have her husband in his helpless misery continue to bless and to adore the God who is torturing him to death. A God so pitiless and so cruel it were better to take leave of than to worship; to renounce his service than to serve him and be requited thus. It were as well to curse him as to bless, for in this desperate extremity it can make matters no worse, for death is equally at hand in either case. Since you must die, die cursing, not blessing, the author of your misery, the source of all our bitter woe.

And thus the loving wife in the frenzy of her anguish has ranged herself unwittingly upon the tempter's side. It is not the first nor only time that fond hearts and friendly hands have unknowingly leagued themselves with the destroyer, and ignorantly done the work of Satan. That Job's wife did what she did under the impulse of her affections seems to be implied in the connection. Her words are introduced as adding force to the temptation and affording a fresh exhibition of the firmness of Job's piety. Cold, unfeeling sarcasm and impious taunt from his wife would not have enticed, but rather repelled. Instead of assailing his integrity at a new and tender point, it would have naturally thrown him into an attitude of resistance to the heartless and wicked suggestion.

But the case is altered, if we see in his wife one who tenderly loves him, and whom he fondly loves. She has stood firmly with him hitherto, but now at length her constancy is overcome; and she would persuade him, too, to abandon his piety, which has not availed to save him from this dismal fate, and to give up the service of a God who, with such a disregard of his constant, faithful worship, has so causelessly and cruelly afflicted him. Job has borne all former disasters unmoved.

His bodily sufferings even cannot shake his integrity. And now the solicitations of his wife he turns aside. His reply to her suggestion is not harsh and severe, as it is frequently interpreted, but rather the language of pained surprise. It is not a stern censure, but a mild rebuke, though decided in its rejection of her ill-judged counsel.

He does not rudely charge her with being herself a foolish woman, whether the meaning be destitute of sense or lacking in true piety. He simply says this was not spoken like herself; it is such a suggestion as he would not have expected from her. She had spoken not with her usual wisdom and pious feeling, but as one of the foolish women speaks. 'Shall we indeed accept good from God, and shall we not accept adversity?' (2:10).

Job's trust in the goodness of the Lord does not falter yet. Here was not, as in his former trial, a simple withdrawal of what God had previously given and in which the amount so withdrawn was simply an index to the goodness of him who had bestowed it. There was now not the mere privation of good, but the positive infliction of evil, of suffering and pain. Job knows not that this suffering encloses a benefit, and is sent with a benevolent design. He cannot therefore praise God for the suffering itself, and acknowledge in it a token of the divine goodness, as he might have done if the lesson had been taught him which the psalmist learned when he said, '*It is* good for me that I have been afflicted' (*Psa.* 119:71), and which the apostle expressed when he said, 'We also glory in tribulations' (*Rom.* 5:3), 'I take pleasure in infirmities, in reproaches, in needs, in persecutions, in distresses for Christ's sake' (*2 Cor.* 12:10). Job did not yet know that all things work together for good to them who love God (*Rom.* 8:28). He did not understand that pain and suffering were or could be anything, else but evils.

Yet regarding them simply in this light, as evils, and evils received from the hand of God, they did not blind him to the fact of the divine goodness and the great preponderance of blessing received from his bountiful hand. The evil does not by any means match the good, much less outweigh it. Shall we forget the immensity of the benefits bestowed because he also sends some suffering? Shall we indeed accept good from God, and shall we not accept adversity?

Job is again victorious, and the tempter is once more foiled. His piety has proved equal to the severity of this fresh test to which it was subjected. 'In all this', the record runs, 'Job did not sin with his lips.'

But Job's trial is not yet ended. He has passed through two stages of it, and has successfully surmounted them. Thus far his piety has borne the test triumphantly, to the confusion of the tempter. He suffered the loss of his property and of his children with noble resignation; with his heart wrung with grief, clad in the insignia of mourning and prostrate on the earth, he still blessed the name of the Lord. He bore the further infliction of what was deemed a fatal disease, accompanied by acute bodily suffering, with heroic fortitude; and though his wife herself threw her weight upon the side of temptation, he still held fast his integrity, and submissively received adversity as well as good from the hand of the Lord. But the third stage of the temptation is yet before him, and it will test his endurance more severely still. It is the persistence of suffering, its continued pressure through long intervals of time.

Many a citadel is proof against assault, which yet may be obliged to succumb to the slow and steady progress of a siege. Constant dropping wears away rocks. There are limits beyond which human endurance cannot go. The first onset of pain and suffering is not nearly so formidable as its protracted continuance, which wears out the strength and uses up the capacity of resistance. Pain which can be patiently borne for a short time becomes intolerable after a longer period.

Sad indeed is the condition of the worn and weary sufferer, whose strength is exhausted, his spirits sunk, his buoyancy gone, all hope fled; unable to calm his irritated nerves or ease his aching limbs, restless and unquiet, finding no repose, no comfortable posture and no cessation of pain, just wearing out the tiresome hours as they drag heavily along; through all the tedious night, and night after night watching for the dawn, which in its turn brings no relief; and through all the day sighing for the night, though the night brings no repose. It is not so much the amount of pain endured at any one moment as its long and wearisome continuance that is so hard to bear. This weary, exhausting round of suffering, with no prospect of relief, is the third stage of Job's heavy trial. The tempter, who had twice failed in his fierce onset, would now wear him out, if possible, and break his strength by continued endurance.

Day after day, week after week, he is still compelled to drag his heavy burden, and he does so in silence. How long we know not. It was some time after his seizure before his friends arrived to comfort him. Doubtless a number of days had passed before they heard of his calamity. A further interval was consumed in concerting an appointment to come. When they arrived, his disease had already so altered his features and form that they lifted up their eyes and knew him not. And after their arrival they sat with him seven days and seven nights before Job uttered a word of lamentation.

Through all this protracted period he bore his grief in silence. But at length his sorrows grow beyond his power to suppress them, and he breaks forth in the piteous moanings of intolerable anguish. He has borne the torture with pious fortitude, until at length nature can hold out no more: he can endure it no longer, and he gives vent to the most distressed sighs and groans; but in it all observe that he does not rail against God.

In the most passionate manner he utters his wailing cry. With the most vehement expressions he heaps execrations on the day in which he was born; he wishes that day blotted from existence – in other words, that it had never been – so that it could not have inflicted upon him the misery of an intolerable existence.

Oh that he had never been born! Oh that when born he had perished, neglected and uncared for, and thus might never have come to know the wretchedness of living! Oh if he had but found in early infancy a grave, which closes over all alike, and sweeps into its all-devouring maw the rich and great, kings and counsellors, the prisoner and the oppressor, the master and his slave, gathering all into that profound and undisturbed repose, which now is denied to him! Oh, how he longs for death! he would clutch at it as the miser grasps his gold, as men dig for hidden treasures. Why is this coveted privilege of death denied him?

Thus the poor sufferer bemoans his dismal fate. It is the doleful lament of one who has more laid upon him than he can bear. It is not the utterance of considerate reflection. It is not the expression of deliberate views. The sentences are not to be nicely weighed, and their propriety or impropriety passed upon as though they were spoken in moments of calm repose. They must be judged of from the situation of Job.

They are the language of one tortured beyond endurance, who cannot support the anguish that he suffers, and whose life has become an intolerable burden. Allowance must be made for these paroxysms of helpless, hopeless sorrow. His strength was not the strength of stones, nor his flesh of brass. He was incapable himself of weighing what he uttered. It only represents the bitterness of irrepressible woe. Still, bruised as he is, hopeless of good, with but one wish, and this that he might die, Job does not reproach or revile his Maker. The tempter has broken his spirit, and crushed him to the earth; but he has not succeeded yet in wresting from him his integrity or bringing him to forsake his God.

Here we must leave the patriarch for the present. This third, most dreadful stage of his trial is not yet ended. The tempter has not relaxed his hold. He has new instruments of torture to apply to the victim already reduced to so pitiable a condition; and he will use them mercilessly. He sees his advantage in Job's extremity of misery, and he will push it to the bitter end, if so he can wring from him the renunciation of his trust in God. Will he be able to compass his malicious design? The future will reveal. Meanwhile let it be recorded that he has not succeeded yet. In the desperate straits to which he has been driven, Job has not yet renounced the service of the Lord.

And may he whose grace supported Job in all his dreadful trials hitherto grant like grace to us – grace according to our need, grace to do according to the measure of the task required of us, grace to bear according to the measure of the burden laid upon us. And to his name be praise. Amen.

5

Job's Three Friends

Now when Job's three friends heard of all this adversity that had come upon him, each one came from his own place – Eliphaz the Temanite, Bildad the Shuhite, and Zophar the Naamathite. For they had made an appointment together to come and mourn with him, and to comfort him (Job 2:11).

Job's sorrows seemed to have reached their last extreme. And now some new persons are introduced upon the scene, who are to be quite conspicuous in the remainder of the book. Three friends meet by appointment at the house of the suffering patriarch, to console and to comfort him. The prominence accorded to them from this point onward shows that their visit is no unimportant incident, but that it is a fact of great consequence in the transaction here recorded. A very large space, and indeed the greater portion of the book, is occupied with what they say to Job, which is here reported in detail, and with what he says in reply. We cannot be mistaken in supposing that they have much to do with the case here pending. They are not mere spectators in a scene which deeply affects them as concerning their intimate and life-long friend. They are themselves actors and participants, and that in a most significant and important way. They appear in the very crisis of Job's trial; in the last and most terrible stage of his sufferings, and when it would seem as though nature could bear no more.

They, too, are unwittingly taken into the service of the tempter, who makes use of them to add a fresh aggravation to Job's intolerable woe, which is most artfully contrived to drive him to that result which Satan seeks to bring about, to make him do what his cunning and unscrupulous enemy has from the first been aiming to bring about, namely to renounce the service of the Lord.

The alternate discourses of the friends and of Job are not simply a discussion of the mysterious subject of God's afflictive dispensations. They are not to be sundered from the circumstances in which they are uttered, which preclude an abstract treatment of a general theme. They are occupied with the case of Job, and every word uttered by his friends finds its way to the sufferer's heart.

He is wounded by their harshness, stung by their censures, exasperated by their reproaches, and driven into antagonism by their arguments. They are the professed advocates of religious obligation. They represent the cause of God, enforcing his claims on Job and justifying his ways with him, which they do in a spirit that repels him, with assumptions that experience does not sanction, and which his own inner consciousness falsifies. The unfairness, if not disingenuousness, with which they plead God's cause, place him under additional temptation to reject that cause itself.

The insoluble conflict which they assume or create between God's justice and Job's integrity, for which he has the testimony of his own conscience and cannot surrender or falsify, tends to place before his mind a distorted image of the character of God. God appears to be torturing him for crimes which he has not committed, to be relentlessly pursuing him as an implacable foe, and without justice or reason to be

employing his resistless power to crush him to the earth. This
is the phantom which his friends are constantly setting before
him, this false notion of God as unjust and pitiless toward
him; and this for which he cannot himself otherwise account,
his own intolerable sufferings seem to rivet upon him. This
phantom, apparently so real, he is incessantly obliged to fight
or it would drive him to absolute despair and force him to
give up his confidence and trust in God and thus throw him
completely into the tempter's snare.

This is the point around which the conflict in Job's soul so
fearfully rages, which is depicted in this book in its various
phases with such a master hand. This is the very acme and
crisis of the temptation. This unwelcome apparition, which
his friends are constantly bringing up and dressing out before
him, of a God of arbitrary power, whose justice, as they
assert it, would be rank injustice, and who seems to be devoid
of pity – this it is which fills him with the deepest anguish.

And yet, in the darkness and the mystery of his unexplained sufferings, how is he to rid himself of it? How to
chase the dreaded spectre away? To admit this conception of
God, which both his own helpless misery and the
arguments and assertions of his friends appear to force upon
him, is to fall inevitably away from God's service. Such a God
might be dreaded; but it is impossible that he could be either
loved or feared.

Here, then, are Job's three friends who, as the self-
constituted advocates of God and the advisers of Job, are
concerned about his spiritual good. They are busily engaged
in letting fly their poisoned arrows and flinging their
envenomed darts. And here is Job himself exposed without
shield or buckler to their dangerous attacks. Can he sustain
the weight of this new burden? Can he hold out against this
fresh assault? Can his confidence in God remain unshaken
when every prop is removed and the very foundations seem
to be swept away? His heart is all laid open before us, down
to its lowest depths, in his discourses with his friends. Every
thing is faithfully photographed. We see all the tumult of

his soul in its conflicting emotions. We see him now sinking, now rising; now almost gone, tottering on the very verge of the precipice, over which to fall would be fatal; now recoiling in the energy of his still unvanquished faith; giving vent to expressions wrung from him in the bitterness of his spirit, which he would not have uttered in calmer moments, until we almost dread to have him open his mouth again, lest he should in his desperation be betrayed into speaking the fatal word to which Satan by all this combination of forces is ceaselessly urging him, and apparently shutting him up.

He is beside himself with intolerable anguish, the terrors of God driving him to distraction, yet through it all he is still ever and anon turning unto God and tearfully looking up to him, his only hope and solace. Can even Job's piety still hold out? Shall the tempter at length succeed?

In order that we may the better understand how and to what extent the friends of Job aggravated his temptation, it will be necessary to pay more particular attention to the persons of these friends, and their conduct and language towards Job. This is the purpose of the present chapter.

The censure which the LORD himself passes upon Job's friends at the close of the book, and the fact that they misapprehend, as they do, the cause of Job's sufferings and the purpose of God's dealings with him, has often led to an undue depreciation of their character. Against this we must carefully guard, or we shall weaken the force of the temptation so far as they are concerned, which lies greatly in this – that such men take part in it, and that they do this to the extent that they do.

We have reason to believe that these were eminent men, wise men, and good men. They were cherished and familiar friends of Job, such as he would naturally lean upon in a time of trouble, or turn to in perplexity for counsel and advice.

They were venerable men, men of age and experience. Eliphaz says to Job:

Both the gray-haired and the aged are among us,
Much older than your father (15:10).

We cannot think of Job, with his ten children grown up to manhood and womanhood, as at this time much less than fifty-five or sixty years old. Eliphaz in this statement probably refers to himself, since the precedence is accorded to him among the friends. He in every instance speaks first, and is followed by the others, and may therefore be supposed to be their superior in age. If this be so, and he alludes to himself as 'grey-haired and aged' and 'much older' than Job's father, he must have been at least as old as seventy-five or eighty.

And age commanded reverence, more even then, in the patriarchal period, than with us. It was significant of distinction, when the oldest living ancestor was the chieftain of the clan; when he was the visible lord of his descendants, and the recognized authority looked up to, deferred to, and obeyed in all their families and dependants. It also spoke of wisdom gathered by long experience and observation, when intercourse with men, and acquaintance with things rather than knowledge of books, were the chief sources of information.

The region in which Job's friends resided should also be noted, for it was proverbial for the sagacity of its inhabitants; and it is not unlikely that it is for this reason that the residence of each is particularly mentioned – Eliphaz the Temanite, Bildad the Shuhite, and Zophar the Naamathite.

Teman was famous for its wise men, and their profound, sententious sayings; so was in fact Arabia, or the East, the country to which the other friends likewise belonged. To this well-known reputation of the region the prophet alludes:

Is wisdom no more in Teman?
Has counsel perished from the prudent?
Has their wisdom vanished? (*Jer.* 49:7).

And when the eminent endowments of Solomon were to be exalted by a comparison, the sacred writer says of him: 'Solomon's wisdom excelled the wisdom of all the men of the East and all the wisdom of Egypt' (*1 Kings* 4:30).

And that Job's friends were worthy representatives of a land of sages is shown by their speeches here recorded, which are marked by extensive observation and careful reflection, and abound in beautiful and appropriate illustrations drawn from both nature and experience. Their reasoning is fallacious, indeed, because it was built on false premises, but their arguments are coherent and strongly put.

They fail to convince or to confute Job, but not from any want of skill in advocacy. They prove themselves no mean antagonists and it requires all his address to parry their blows. What saves him is not his superiority in argument, but that it is a matter of personal consciousness about which they contend. No subtleties and no cogency of demonstration can convict him of offences of which his own conscience pronounces him innocent.

They misinterpret the ways of providence, and fail to explain the mystery of Job's sufferings. But this is from no mental incapacity. Job can see no farther into this dark dispensation than they can. But he knows that they are mistaken although he no more understands the real state of the case than they do. The fact is that the enigma is insoluble by the unaided reason of man. God can alone declare the purpose of his afflictive dispensations, and this he had never yet revealed. These distresses of Job were to afford the occasion of shedding the first rays of light upon it. It is no discredit to the friends any more than to Job that they did not discern what they had no means of knowing. In what they really were to blame, and to what extent, we shall inquire presently.

They were, moreover, good men, and had at heart a real affection for Job. The whole tenor of their speeches shows that they were concerned both for the honour of God and for the spiritual welfare of Job. They advocate and approve what is good; they reject and condemn the bad. Their discourses sparkle with gems of morality and religious truth. The principles which they propound are mostly just and unexceptionable as general maxims. It is only the application which they make of them to a case that they do not really cover, which is false. They entertain a true friendship for Job;

but the mistake under which they are with regard to him and his trials warps their judgement; and, in their desire to reclaim him from imaginary wrong-doing, they are themselves guilty of actual though unintended injustice, and treat him with unmerited severity.

The friends of Job, then, as we may conceive, were men of distinction, eminent for wisdom and of approved piety, worthy confidants and intimates of Job, trusted and tried doubtless in the companionship of years. They hear of the great sorrows of their friend, and they show their attachment to him by agreeing to meet at his house to mourn with him and to comfort him. They bring him in actual fact but little comfort, it is true; but this is the design and expectation with which they come.

It is important to observe the change which takes place in the friends themselves in their feelings and attitude towards Job in the progress of the book. This is depicted with admirable art, and is essential to a proper understanding of the whole transaction. To impute to them from the beginning the harsh and ungenerous suspicions which they come to entertain and express towards the last, is to mistake their character entirely, to confuse what is perfectly distinct, and to lose sight of that inward change in their sentiments respecting Job which is so skilfully drawn and is so true to nature. The longer the friends argue with him without convincing him, the more obdurate and incorrigible he appears to them, and the more severe is the censure which they are disposed to pass upon him.

They come with sympathy and sorrow for him in his griefs. Finding him so changed that they no longer recognize him, they are affected to tears. 'They lifted their voices and wept; and each one tore his robe and sprinkled dust on his head toward heaven. So they sat down with him on the ground seven days and seven nights, and no one spoke a word to him, for they saw that his grief was very great' (2:12–13). They could not more tenderly and delicately express their commiseration for him in his terrible sorrows, which it was beyond the power of human helpers to mitigate or to relieve. In all this there was genuine pity and compassion. There is no room for supposing that they entertained any other than the most friendly feelings, or that any ungenerous suspicions had as yet taken possession of their minds as to the reality of Job's piety or the reasons of these extraordinary sufferings which had been sent upon him.

Job first breaks the mournful silence by his outburst of lamentation, extorted by insupportable distress. Eliphaz, probably the eldest and most respected of the three friends, as he is certainly the most dignified and courteous in his style of address, first makes reply. And, as Job answers him, he is successively followed by Bildad and by Zophar.

As the interview still proceeds, and Job continues to respond, the friends once more address themselves to him in the same order; and yet again the third time. Only in the third and last series of discourses the third friend, Zophar, fails to speak, for a reason to be stated hereafter.

Eliphaz and Bildad accordingly each speak three times, and Zophar twice, Job invariably responding. There is thus a triple series of discourses, in which the growing alienation and distrust of the friends can be plainly traced. They begin with comparative mildness and expressions of regard. But, as the discussion advances, they are astounded and roused by Job's opposition to what they esteem primary principles of religious faith; they are provoked and incensed by his obstinacy, his want of submission to the divine allotment, and by his language, which appears to them to savour of irreverence and impiety; until at length they lose all confidence in his uprightness and sincerity, and believe him to have been secretly guilty of the most atrocious crimes.

When Job, unable to contain himself under the pressure of his anguish, utters his wail of frantic grief, cursing the day in which he was born, and complaining that life with all its miseries is forced upon him, when he would so gladly be blotted from existence or seek rest in the grave, Eliphaz feels called upon to interpose a remonstrance. He makes an endeavour in this first speech to rouse his friend from this utter despondency, to remind him of the moral reasons of this terrible affliction, and to exhort him to that more complete submission which would be followed by the return of God's favour, and by more than his former prosperity.

He begins in an apologetic and sensitive strain:

If one attempts a word with you, will you become weary?
But who can withhold himself from speaking? (4:2)

He then proceeds by bidding Job remember how he had strengthened and comforted others in their affliction and so, he ought not now to show weakness himself. As a good and righteous man, he should not be despondent, but hope in God, who would not suffer the innocent to perish, nor the righteous to be cut off.

As to the source of his troubles, he reminds him of the universal sinfulness of men. Mortal man cannot be just in the sight of God, nor man pure before his Maker. Men are sinners; hence their frail and perishable nature. They are crushed before the moth, they are destroyed from morning to evening. Affliction does not come forth from the dust, neither do troubles spring out of the ground. They arise from no extraneous sources. But man is born to trouble as the sparks fly upward. He is involved in it by a necessity of his nature: it springs directly out of his inborn sinfulness.

Hence Eliphaz admonishes Job to submit his case humbly and trustfully to God, under whose universal and righteous providence the poor has hope, and iniquity is compelled to stop her mouth.

He shall deliver you in six troubles,
Yes, in seven no evil shall touch you (5:19).

And he concludes by describing in beautiful and impressive terms the happy consequences of submissively accepting the LORD's correction.

To this plausible and, rhetorically considered, elegant address of Eliphaz, there are two exceptions to be taken. In the first place, it could not but grate harshly on the ears of

Job that his friend should expect him to sustain his long-continued and bitter sufferings with equanimity, and that he should appear to reproach him with not himself exhibiting that fortitude now in his own case which he had inculcated in that of others as if there were no limits to human endurance, and it were possible to bear up under misery like his without a word of complaint.

The sobs and groans and lamentations wrung from him by an anguish too severe to be quietly endured is surely a weakness that is not to be too harshly judged. And the appeal to Job's piety, as though this should have quieted his clamour and led him still to maintain a cheerful hope amidst his overwhelming distress, showed a want of consideration for the condition in which he then was. There was in all this a lack of that tenderness and that appreciative sympathy which was a prime requisite in one who would comfort such a mourner as Job.

The second point open to exception in the discourse of Eliphaz is not a matter of feeling, like the preceding, but of principle. It is the manner in which he represents sin and suffering as linked together in God's providential dispensations, as though this afforded an adequate explanation of every case of affliction, Job's included.

This point is so skilfully put, that what he actually says can scarcely be objected to: it is only what he implies, by offering this as the solution of the case in hand. He brings no harsh or doubtful charge against Job. He expresses no suspicion, and apparently entertains none, about the depth and reality of his piety. His plea is rather based on the assumption that Job is really what he has ever been supposed to be in uprightness and the devout fear of God.

He lays no accusation upon him but such as is common to all who are sharers of our degenerate nature. All are impure in the sight of God, and all are in consequence born to trouble. As exposure to suffering, and suffering itself, is an inevitable result of that corrupt nature with which we were born, the wise and reasonable course, and the truly pious course, is not to indulge in passionate outcries against the divine orderings, which can only be productive of harm to the sufferer himself (5:2), but meekly to accept and submit to the sorrows which he sends, who makes sore and binds up, who wounds and his hands make whole. Such submission will surely lead to peace and to salvation.

It is undoubtedly true that where there is no sin there will be no suffering among the subjects of God's moral government. All suffering has sin as its invariable and necessary antecedent. It is also true that the consciousness of sin and ill-desert must for ever close the mouth of every sufferer from any well-grounded complaint against the righteousness of God. The holiest and the best are sinners nevertheless; and, whatever sufferings they may endure in the providence of God, it cannot be said that they are unjustly treated; for, as Zophar states this point in more developed form to Job, 'God exacts from you *less* than your iniquity *deserves*' (11:6). No man's sufferings in this world are equal to his just deserts.

But, while this is true and incontestable, it does not account for cases of special and extraordinary suffering, and especially such as occur in the experience of good men such as Job. The general sinfulness of men may account for human sorrows so far as they are uniformly distributed; and a like principle may be applied where they are plainly graduated in proportion to the demerit of the sufferers. But special suffering, not involving special guilt, cannot be thus accounted for. A sinfulness common to all cannot be the reason why one is singled out rather than another, and made to endure extraordinary sorrows.

The special significance of suffering, therefore, remains unexplained. Its importance as a test of character, its value as a means of discipline and training, and the far more exceeding reward by which it shall be abundantly compensated, are not once considered. Eliphaz alleges that man suffers because he is a sinner; he knew not that a man may likewise suffer because he is a saint that he may thus exhibit more distinctly his saintly character; that he may be ripened still more in holiness; and that his final recompense may be proportionally increased. Suffering, to Eliphaz, was ever and only a punishment, a judgement for sin, an infliction of the divine displeasure. He knew not that it might also be a token of love, a means of grace, a blessing in disguise; that whom the LORD loves he chastens, and scourges every son whom he receives.

The other friends, in their discourses, follow Eliphaz in the principles and method of the discussion, only with increased vehemence and more open censure of Job. Their axiom is that God cannot deal unjustly, and therefore suffering must be the fruit of sin.

Bildad intimates that Job's children had but suffered the consequences of their own misdeeds, so that this loss which he had experienced was the result of sin, not his own indeed, but theirs; and he puts an 'if' before his affirmation of the piety of Job himself:

> If you would earnestly seek God
> And make your supplication to the Almighty,
> If you *were* pure and upright,
> Surely now he would awake for you,
> And prosper your rightful dwelling place (8:5–6).

Zophar puts the 'if' before the contrary hypothesis as to Job's character and conduct, implying at least its possibility:

> If iniquity *were* in your hand, *and you* put it far away,
> And would not let wickedness dwell in your tents;
> Then surely you could lift up your face without spot;
> Yes, you could be steadfast, and not fear;
> Because you would forget *your* misery,
> And remember *it* as waters *that have* passed away,
> And your life would be brighter than noonday.
> *Though* you were dark, you would be like the morning
> (11:14–17).

The vividness and beauty of the imagery which they employ, and the force and vigour of their expressions, cannot fail to charm and to impress, however unsatisfactory their treatment of the mystery with which they deal, however unsound or rather one-sided the conclusions to which they come, and however unjust and ungenerous they may be in their treatment of Job.

When Eliphaz speaks a second time, it is plain that he has undergone a considerable change in his feelings towards Job. He reasserts the fundamental principle, common to him and the other friends, of the necessary connection of suffering with sin. But he no longer illustrates or defends it by the consideration of the universal and native sinfulness of the race. It is not of man as 'born to trouble' that he now speaks, so much as of man 'who drinketh iniquity like water'.

It is the fate of the ungodly and the wicked man that he holds up before Job for his warning. And instead of presupposing Job's integrity and urging him in consequence to cherish the hope that he should not be utterly cut off, he charges him rather with serious guilt; not, it is true, with criminal misdeeds or acts of sin, but with wicked words. In his speeches now uttered in the presence of the friends he has inculpated himself. He has maintained principles and uttered expressions inconsistent with pious reverence for God:

> Yes, you cast off fear,
> And restrain prayer before God (15:4).

That is to say, you put an end to piety and annul the value of prayer by the sentiments which you have here propounded.

> For your iniquity teaches your mouth,
> And you choose the tongue of the crafty.
> Your own mouth condemns you, and not I;
> Yes, your own lips testify against you (15:5–6).

Bildad and Zophar once more follow Eliphaz in the same general strain, holding up before Job the destruction that is certain, sooner or later, to overtake the ungodly, and intimating, not obscurely, that this is the explanation of the dismal fate which has befallen him.

Eliphaz in his third discourse makes a yet further advance. He now, without any ambiguity of language or indirectness of intimation, explicitly, and in so many terms, charges Job with the most atrocious wickedness. He has become more and more estranged from him as the discussion has proceeded. He has become more and more convinced from the language of Job himself that he is destitute of real piety, until at length all his former confidence in him has utterly vanished, and he not only believes him capable of any amount of wickedness, but is persuaded that he has actually perpetrated crimes of the most serious character, and that the sorrows by which he has so suddenly and so fearfully been overwhelmed are thus easily accounted for.

It is not now the general sinfulness of human nature which he adduces against him as in his first discourse. Nor does he merely allege the language of impiety and irreverence to be found in his speeches which he had here uttered in their presence, as in his second discourse. Nor does he content himself with indirect insinuations and implications that his fate was but the customary fate of the wicked, as the other friends had already done. But he goes beyond all this, and makes open and direct charges of habitual and gross transgression:

> *Is* not your wickedness great,
> And your iniquity without end?
> For you have taken pledges from your brother for no reason,
> And stripped the naked of their clothing.
> You have not given the weary water to drink,
> And you have withheld bread from the hungry . . .
> You have sent widows away empty,
> And the strength of the fatherless was crushed.
> Therefore snares are all around you,
> And sudden fear troubles you (22:5–7, 9).

A just and all-seeing God has detected the villainy and set the brand of his reprobation upon it. Job was suffering just what might be expected as the righteous recompense of the iniquity which he had practised. His fancied impunity is now at an end, and deserved vengeance has overtaken him at last. What a spectacle is this! And what a lesson it reads to us! This man is one whom God declared to be without his equal for piety in the earth – blameless and upright, and one who feared God and shunned evil. And yet here are good men, wise men, men of age and experience, his friends and intimates through many former years, knowing him not merely by reputation but by personal, familiar, and long acquaintance, who do not scruple to cherish the grossest and most unjust suspicions, and actually to charge upon him the most egregious misconduct. And all this they do without the slightest foundation in actual fact. It is purely inferential and suppositional; nevertheless they charge it upon him as though they had the most undoubted evidence of its reality. We say again, what a spectacle! And what a lesson it reads to us!

The friends of Job, as has been admitted already, are not to blame for not knowing what could only be known by divine revelation, and had not then been revealed. It neither implies any obliquity of moral vision, nor any dullness of intellectual perception, that they were unable to discern the true intent of the sufferings of Job, or the divine purpose in permitting them. This was a secret still undisclosed. The mystery of the afflictions of the righteous was now to be unveiled as it had not been before; and the sufferings of Job were to furnish the occasion, by the lessons to be divinely communicated in connection with this event.

But this was not to be done until gifted minds, and well instructed in the general truths of religion before made known, had first employed themselves upon it, and shown by the trial the incompetency of unaided reason to solve the riddle, or to dissipate the darkness which overhung the dispensation. The ignorance of Job's friends, and of Job himself, regarding the meaning and design of God's dealings with him, was not reprehensible. This could not have been otherwise, for they had no means of knowing it.

So far then they are excusable. But what cannot be excused in them is that in the first place they undertook to expound, as though they had full knowledge in the case, what they did not understand; and in so doing based the divine procedure on insufficient reasons, and sought to square it by their own limited notions. If they had confessed the mystery and owned their ignorance regarding it, all would have been well. They would have been saved from their subsequent errors and mistakes, and from the gross injustice of which they were guilty towards Job.

By acting as they did, they in fact arraigned the providence of God, which they were professedly defending. They prescribed a rule for its administration as the only one compatible with justice, which is not, after all, the method which it actually follows. Suffering is not distributed according to the ratio nor on the principles which they allege to be absolutely demanded by God's essential attributes. By defending his dispensations on grounds which are demonstrably inadequate, and insisting that these are the grounds on which their defence must necessarily be rested, they do, in fact, proclaim that these dispensations are indefensible; and they do their utmost, unwittingly indeed, but no less really, to bring them into discredit.

And in the second place they were inexcusable in another respect. They not only entered a weak and unsuitable plea as the only one upon which the cause of God could be based or his providence justified, but they likewise undertook to bolster up his cause by a disingenuous, if not positively immoral method.

As Job charges upon them (13:7), they spoke wickedly for God, and talked deceitfully for him. They made allegations which they had no means of knowing to be true, and which, in fact, were not true: they were mere inferences from the false premises on which they were conducting the defence of the divine government.

In defending the cause of religion and of piety, as they professed to do, they were guilty of making rash and reckless assertions; they were unjust to Job in not only harbouring baseless suspicions, but in venturing on positive declarations of his guilt in matters of which he was wholly innocent; they were shamefully cruel to their suffering friend, causelessly aggravating his distress, which, professedly, they had come to soothe, when he was already weighed down by troubles that might have disarmed malice itself and softened hearts of stone.

No exigencies of their argument could justify a course like this. And no limits in which the defence of God's righteous government and the claims of religion seemed to be, could justify it. If the divine administration could not be honestly and truthfully defended, without a resort to what is questionable or false, they should have retired from its defence, and concluded that they were not called of God to be his champions in this particular. They should have owned the mystery and confessed their ignorance, and waited patiently till the LORD himself disclosed the impregnable basis on which he chose to have his cause rested. Confiding in him who does great things and unsearchable, and whose ways are past finding out, they should have trusted that he would make all plain in his own good time, instead of presuming to put forth unholy hands to support the ark of God, and darkening his infinite counsel by words without knowledge.

The gross charges put forth by Eliphaz could not be repeated by Bildad in his speech next following, in the face of Job's solemn asseveration of his innocence, and his appeal to the omniscient judge of all. He accordingly recedes from them entirely, and falls back upon the original position of Eliphaz in his opening speech namely the universal sinfulness of men, in which Job is of necessity involved. He thus not only retracts the charges hitherto insinuated or openly made against Job, but concedes his inability to conduct the argument further. He has nothing to adduce but what had been adduced and answered long before. The same thing is likewise intimated by the brevity of his speech, which consists of but a few commonplace sentences. And Zophar makes no attempt to speak at all. He has nothing whatever to say.

The friends accordingly give up their argument with Job. They cannot convince or confute him. They entered their protest against his complaint in his wild outburst of grief.

They sought to convict him of the irreverence and impiety of which they thought him guilty, and to bring him back to what they esteemed right views and a proper spirit. Instead of this they, in point of fact, threw themselves upon the side of the great adversary. They became the tools and accomplices of Satan in his sore temptation, giving all their weight to the scale opposed to God and goodness, embittering Job against a cause which was upheld by such disingenuous methods, and by methods so unjust to himself.

They cast discredit upon God's providence, which was so inadequately defended and justified by arguments which were palpably false; and tempted Job to renounce the service of God himself, whom they represented in a light that served only to repel.

The question has now reached its utmost intensity. Can Job withstand the temptation which is brought to bear upon him with all this accumulated force? With his property swept away; his children gone; himself the victim of a loathsome and painful disorder; his very wife entreating him to abandon the service of a God so cruel, the author of all their woes; his agony, both of body and of mind, still growing, without the prospect of release; the trusted friends of former years deserting and scorning him, and stinging him with their undeserved reproaches; while he is himself totally unable to comprehend the righteousness or the reasons of this dreadful infliction – can he bear it all and still maintain his trust in God, who hides himself in such awful darkness?

The answer is to be found in Job's successive replies to his friends, in which all the workings of his soul in this fearful crisis are so vividly and faithfully portrayed. The examination of these replies must be deferred until another chapter.

Meanwhile, may he, who alone can, in mercy uphold and comfort all his tried and suffering saints. Amen.

6

Job's Conflict

My friends scorn me; My eyes pour out tears to God (Job 16:20).

Satan now has his trail completely laid; and it would almost seem as though at length he has his victim entirely in his power and there was no escape out of the fatal snare. Job, with all he had, was put at the disposal of the evil one, with the single limitation that he must spare his life. And Satan has used the liberty accorded to him without stint. He has brought the most frightful complication of sorrows and sufferings upon the unsuspecting patriarch, and set every influence at work that he could bring to bear upon him, to overturn his integrity and detach him from the service of God. Can he succeed in his fiendish purpose?

He has crushed the spirit of Job, and quenched his hopes. He has accumulated pain and grief upon him, until, in the depth of his long-continued anguish, existence itself has become an insupportable burden. The weary sufferer, stunned, bewildered, tortured to the last extreme of despair, curses the day that he was born, and longs for nothing so much as to die.

It would seem as though nature could hold out no longer. Satan perceives his advantage in this crisis of Job's misery, and presses it relentlessly, through the medium of his friends, who unwittingly range themselves on the tempter's side. These professed ministers of consolation and advocates of piety treat him in a manner which embitters him against them and the cause which they defend.

Their pleas for the equity of the divine administration are repugnant to his sense of right, and to the testimony of his own conscience. They represent his aggravated sufferings as a righteous retribution, either for the sinfulness inborn in our common human nature, or for the sin, betrayed in his present irreverent and unsubmissive speeches, or for the guilt of some gross criminality now first detected and brought to light.

These assumptions Job repels point by point. His sufferings cannot be so explained. What, then, is the inevitable alternative? Is not God unrighteous? Is he not treating him as an offender, when he knows him to be innocent? Or is he not at least like an implacable foe, mercilessly and gratuitously inflicting upon him these grievous sorrows? If woe like this be not the award of justice, must it not be injustice or wanton cruelty? And, if God be either unjust or pitiless, how can the sufferer, crushed beneath his arbitrary inflictions, adore or trust him?

Job's triumph is, in the most absolute and unqualified manner, the triumph of faith over sense. He seems to outward view to have no ground left to stand upon. Satan has apparently shut him up to conclusions respecting the providence of God, which positively exclude worship and piety. It would seem as though everything conspired to show God was persecuting him, and treating him as an enemy. Yet from an angry God he can turn nowhere but back to God himself, in whom he does and must confide, in spite of his apparent hostility. God is still his only refuge, even from the fierceness of his own displeasure:

Though He slay me, yet will I trust Him (13:15).

Job's triumph was not easily gained. He was indeed severely beset by the adversary. The struggle was desperate, and tested his constancy to the utmost. The contest was not barely one of fortitude, of capacity to endure, of power to bear up under calamities and sufferings, and to rise superior to that terrible combination of distresses which was weighing him down.

The question to be settled was not whether Job had that heroic firmness, and indomitable self-mastery and self-control, or rather self-sufficiency, which was the Stoic's ideal, and could calmly bear all outward losses, and support undisturbed the most grievous inflictions of pain and sorrow. His trial lay in a totally different plane. The point of it was whether he would still cleave to God and maintain his trust in him when there no longer remained anything external to attract him to his service, but everything combined to repel him and drive him from it.

The hand of God was in these dreadful sorrows. Why had he sent them, or permitted them? The Christian can readily answer this question, and can comprehend without difficulty how afflictions are consistent with the divine goodness and love. But the revelations which shed such a cheerful light for us upon this mysterious subject had not then been given. Job was left to confront the difficulty, with no help afforded him for its solution.

He was in utter darkness and perplexity, and unable to apprehend the reasons of the dispensation. And the only solution which offered itself, and towards which he was persistently driven by antagonism to the inadmissible position urged upon him by his friends, was not reconcilable with the goodness or justice of God.

Hence the tumult of his soul, and the tempest of conflicting emotions which rages within him. Reason and sense urge him in one direction, and the strong recoil of faith drives him back in the other; and thus he is swayed perpetually to and fro, still hoping against hope, ever afresh seeking unto God who had cast him off, unable to release himself from the toils which Satan had so artfully woven around him, yet continuing to struggle, and never submitting to be captured; unable to escape from conclusions to which the logic of his sufferings seemed to constrain him, or to banish the forbidding spectre of an angry God which they perpetually raise before him, and yet holding fast to his inmost convictions, in spite of all that seems to contradict them.

This inward struggle of Job is not made the subject of any formal description; but it is vividly depicted in his successive speeches in reply to his friends. These lay bare all the workings of his soul, and the fearful agitation which was going on within him.

They disclose the terrible conflict through which he was passing, in its various phases, until out of the depths of despair he fought his way to solid peace. They show into what distress the tempter plunged him; what gloom and darkness had settled upon his path; to what spiritual straits he was reduced; but how in spite of all he never abandoned his faith in God.

He staggered and tottered under the tremendous blows which were given him, and it seemed at times as though he could not recover himself, and must fall. But somehow he always regained his footing, and never lost his balance entirely. The adversary was foiled, notwithstanding all his arts and all the weapons he employed. And the piety of Job, which he sought to undermine or to destroy, sustained the test, and triumphed in the encounter.

Job's opening speech, in which he first breaks his silence and pours forth his piteous plaint of woe, is a soliloquy. It is the melancholy wail of insupportable anguish. It is the frantic outburst of grief, which has been held in until it can no longer be repressed, and to which he now gives vent, apparently unconscious that any one is present, bemoaning himself without the thought of being overheard. The burden of his speech is the misery of this intolerable existence: Oh that I had never lived! Oh that now I might cease to be!

When Eliphaz and the other friends undertake to address him, reproving him for his want of submission, justifying the dispensation under which he suffers, and pointing out what they conceive to be the true method of relief, Job directs his replies partly to them and partly to God. He speaks to his friends with the double aim of arousing their pity and replying to their arguments.

What he says to God is likewise of a twofold character: He both wrestles with God, expostulating with him for the misery which he has inflicted upon him, and he affirms his confidence in him. It is in these addresses to God that his inward agony most fully asserts itself; that the antagonistic emotions with which his soul is rent asunder meet in the sharpest contrast and collision; and that he undergoes the greatest and most sudden transitions of feeling.

The progress and the stages of Job's inward strife are very plainly marked. His ineffectual appeals to his friends for the sympathy which they deny him throw him back more and more upon God, as his only source of help. Refused the pity that he craves on earth, he can look nowhere but to heaven, and is forced to seek his only refuge there.

Accordingly, that which overwhelmingly occupies his mind in the first instance is the relation between himself and God. Is God his enemy, or is he his friend? Despair and hope struggle for the mastery, and the conflict grows more and more intense until the climax is reached at the central point of the discussion between him and his friends.

Corresponding to the three series of speeches addressed to Job by his three friends, who follow each other in the same invariable order, are the three series of his replies severally addressed to them.

Throughout the first series of Job's rejoinders, and into the middle of the second the conflict in his soul continues to heighten, until in his second reply to his second friend, Bildad, it attains its acme. Here the opposing principles come to their most intense encounter. His sense of the hostility of God to him reaches its most vivid and vehement expression, but it is immediately succeeded and swallowed up by the conviction which overspreads his soul of the certainty of God's friendship and favour, which, though the worst comes to the worst, must and will manifest itself, hereafter if not now, in the world to come, if not in this. With this burst of triumph the temptation is trodden under foot. Satan is vanquished, and Job's inward conflict is substantially over. Faith has gotten the victory. He has gained the assurance that God is his Redeemer, come what may and in spite of all adverse appearances. And with this the whole power of the temptation is broken.

But the darkness is not dispersed. The mystery of the dispensation is no nearer its solution. The enigma remains, and is as inexplicable as ever. Why he has been made to suffer or allowed to suffer so terribly he does not know. He has not the faintest idea of the reason of the affliction. He does not discern how it is to be reconciled with the goodness of God, or his righteousness, or his favour towards himself.

But he has laid hold of the fact with the strong grasp of faith that God is his Redeemer and his friend; and his confident trust does not again give way. Notwithstanding the continuance of his sufferings and the difficulties that encumber their explanation, he is now on the solid rock. The floods may dash around him, but they cannot break over him; and he is no longer in peril of being overwhelmed.

Having thus reached comparative peace, and settled the question which chiefly agitated him hitherto – of his relation to God – Job next turns his attention more immediately to his controversy with his friends. He has denied the truth of their position before, and stated facts at variance with it; but in his subsequent speeches, namely the last of the second series and in those of the third series, he refutes their position by reviewing their arguments in detail, and he shows that they have furnished no adequate or satisfactory account whether of God's providence in general or of his sorrows in particular.

Having thus hastily sketched in outline the current of Job's feelings toward God and his attitude toward his friends, we may now return to take a more deliberate survey of his several speeches, with the view of noting more minutely his demeanour at each successive step of his great struggle.

In his first reply to Eliphaz, Job is in the same state of

unrelieved despair as in his opening complaint. The poor alleviation even of the sympathy of his friends had been denied him, and he bitterly upbraids them for withholding that pity which was so needful to him in his distressed situation, and would have cost them so little.

Eliphaz had reminded him of the infinite greatness of God, and of the feebleness and frailty of sinful man, and urged these as reasons why he should be submissive under his sufferings. To Job's mind these are but an aggravation of his misery and a fresh justification of his complaint. He had but one brief life to live, and this was filled up with weariness and woe:

> Therefore I will not restrain my mouth;
> I will speak in the anguish of my spirit;
> I will complain in the bitterness of my soul (7:11).

And he converts these into pleas with the Almighty that he would mitigate the severity of his treatment. He was too insignificant and frail, sinner though he was, to deserve or to require such terrible constancy of attention from the infinite God. It was making too much of a creature so trifling and so powerless that he should be so fearfully visited, and made a mark at which God was always directing his shafts, and never allowed a moment's respite day or night, when he would shortly sleep in the dust and cease to be.

There does not appear to be a single ray of comfort nor a gleam of hope for the stricken sufferer in the present or the future, from man or from God. But from this abyss of darkness and cheerless despondancy he struggles constantly upward towards the light.

In each successive speech some slight advance is made; there is each time some fresh reaching out towards help or hope. Every address made by his friends shows him more and more plainly that nothing is to be looked for or expected from them; they still persist in refusing to him even that measure of relief or consolation which human sympathy might supply. Cut off from all earthly assistance or even pity, there is no one but God to whom he can have recourse. And here he is torn by conflicting feelings. God is persecuting and afflicting him, and, to all outward appearance, is treating him as an enemy. And still he cannot let go that inward persuasion, which manifests itself at first but dimly, and yet grows in clearness and strength as he recurs to it, that God will not altogether withhold his favour from him. Each time that he tries to speak, sense and faith stand in blank antagonism. His sufferings press overwhelmingly upon him with their apparent evidence that God is against him. But faith comes with its whispers, scarcely audible, and yet refusing to be stifled, that God must nevertheless be on his side.

These suggestions of his unquenched confidence in God are only hypothetical at first. If such an obstacle were only removed, or if such a condition could only exist, then God would surely manifest himself in his favour. But the obstacle remains; the condition is impossible to be realized; and so he sinks back each time into a state of unrelieved despondency and gloom.

But his despair is no longer absolute and total. These suggestions of faith and hope gradually assume a more definite form, and take upon themselves more reality. They gain in strength, and come to a fuller utterance with each successive response he makes to his friends, until at last they grow into a clear and decided conviction, which dissipates the clouds of despondency, breaks through the toils which the adversary has thrown around him, and vanquishes the temptation completely and forever by the language of triumphant assurance, 'I know that my Redeemer lives' (19:25).

In the reply to Bildad, the second of the friends, we see the first budding of this rising hope, the first glimmer of the coming dawn. We there find the earliest suggestion of a more favourable issue; but it is a suggestion clogged with an impossible condition, and which cannot be realized in the form in which it presents itself to his mind.

If he could but speak with God on equal terms, if God would lay aside his infinite majesty and divest himself of his awful terrors, then he would present his case before him and it would be acceptably heard, and he would be vindicated by his Judge. But how is such a hearing to be obtained?

> For *He* is not a man, as I *am*,
> *That* I may answer Him,
> *And that* we should go to court together.
> Nor is there any mediator between us,
> *Who* may lay his hand on us both' (9:32–33).

He nevertheless pours forth his expostulation with God, pleading with him for his righteousness' sake and for his past mercies, upon which he fondly dwells, not to destroy him.

> I will say to God, 'Do not condemn me;
> Show me why You contend with me.
> *Does it* seem good to You that you should oppress,
> That You should despise the work of Your hands,
> And smile on the counsel of the wicked?' (10:2–3).

When Zophar, the last of the friends, speaks, it is in the same strain with those who had preceded him, only with greater harshness and impetuosity. If Job had entertained a lingering expectation of pity or even justice from at least one of his friends, this is now gone. And he retorts in terms of bitter and indignant rebuke for their arrogant conceit in adducing the familiar common-places of God's rectitude and justice, as though they were an adequate solution of the mysteries of his providence.

These rest on totally different and as yet unexplained grounds. They were undertaking to vindicate God's providence in a manner which would not be sanctioned by God himself. They were justifying the dealings of God by false and unfounded assumptions. They were in fact impugning the righteousness of God, which they professed to defend, for they suspended its defence on the assumption that he invariably acted on principles, upon which he did not even ordinarily act in his administration of human affairs, and upon which Job knew from his own inward consciousness he was not acting in the present instance.

He was confident, therefore, that God would declare in his favour and not in theirs. He was sure of a vindication, if his case could only come before God. And his mind recurs again to the same twofold obstruction as before; and the hypothesis of its removal, though doubtful and distant, does not seem so absolutely impossible as before.

> Only two *things* do not do to me,
> Then I will not hide myself from You:
> Withdraw Your hand far from me,
> And let not the dread of You make me afraid.
> Then call, and I will answer;
> Or let me speak, then You respond to me (13:20–22).

But the sense of his misery returns upon him and of his life almost at an end, cut off amidst his hopeless sufferings; and what possibility remains of a divine vindication?

> For there is hope for a tree,
> If it is cut down, that it will sprout again,
> And that its tender shoots will not cease . . .
> So man lies down and does not rise.
> Till the heavens *are* no more,
> They will not awake
> Nor be roused from their sleep (14:7, 12).

Oh if it were otherwise! If death were but a temporary suspension of his earthly life! If he could go down to the grave for a season, until God's favour were restored to him, and then could return to the land of the living and come back to his former abode, he would patiently bear all that was laid upon him now.

> Oh, that You would hide me in the grave,
> That You would conceal me until Your wrath is past,
> That You would appoint me a set time, and remember me!
> If a man dies, shall he live *again*?
> All the days of my hard service I will wait,
> Till my change comes (14:13–14),

that is, his restoration from death to life.

Job is trembling here on the verge of a hope full of immortality, which is soon to assume its proper form before his mind and to swell to its just dimensions. But it is as yet only inadequately conceived by him. A conscious state of existence beyond the grave was part of the faith of the early patriarchs, who looked forward to being 'gathered to their fathers' (see *Gen.* 49:29; *Judg.* 2:10). But the future state was then revealed only in the most dim and shadowy outline. It was to them an unseen and unknown world; no bright and joyous anticipations were connected with it, no clear disclosures had yet been made regarding it. The bare fact of its reality was almost all that was known.

The veil was about to be lifted to the wrestling soul of Job further than it had ever been raised to human eyes before. The lesson of his immortality was one of special value for his present need. And he is here darkly and vaguely feeling after it, and reaching out towards it. In all his speeches hitherto the grave has been the end of all that he expected or hoped for – not, we may assume the end of being and conscious spiritual existence, but of life in any desirable sense.

He had no anticipations of good in the grave or beyond it, no thought of blessedness in another state which could outweigh or alleviate his present sorrows. All his notions of the future were negative. He conceived of it simply as a state of privation of all earthly good. He had no idea of the positive blessings belonging to it, of its bliss and glory and beatific vision of God. He looked downward to Sheol, the land of ghosts and shades, not upward to heaven, the abode of glorified spirits in the immediate presence of God himself.

The mists that shrouded the future world were never taken completely away until Jesus Christ abolished death and brought life and immortality to light through the gospel. The apostles and disciples of Christ stand in an entirely different attitude to the future world, and hold a different language respecting it from the saints of God who preceded his coming. The consciousness that to die is gain, the desire to depart as far better than to abide in the flesh, belongs wholly to the New Testament. It has no parallel in the Old. Nevertheless, preliminary lessons of great value were already given under the former dispensation. And one of the first gleams of heavenly light sent to irradiate the darkness of the grave is found in this book of Job. It is born of an assurance graciously vouchsafed to his soul as he struggles with his terrible temptation.

In all that he had said hitherto of death, it has been spoken of as terminating every hope and every prospect.

As the cloud disappears and vanishes away,
So he who goes down to the grave does not come up.
He shall never return to his house,
Nor shall his place know him anymore (7:9–10).

Before I go *to the place from which* I shall not return,
To the land of darkness and the shadow of death,
A land as dark as darkness *itself,*
As the shadow of death, without any order,
Where even the light is like darkness (10:21–22).

But in the speech to Zophar upon which we are now remarking, he ventures the hypothetical suggestion of a return again to life from the dead. If that were only possible, it would relieve the gloom of this dark dispensation under which he is suffering. It would allay the strife, which now rages in his soul, between his conviction that God will declare on his behalf and the outward appearance as though God were his foe. It would open the way to a reconciliation between these seeming contradictions. It would afford an opportunity for the divine favour, of which he was inwardly assured, still to manifest itself to him.

In the precise form in which this vague suggestion has arisen in his mind, it cannot be realized. This earthly life cannot again be renewed. And with this impossibility he relapses again into his former state of cheerless despondency. But the germ of hope is there, which will soon unfold itself in a more practicable form to the assured conviction of God's favour manifested to him in a future life.

The temptation is now approaching its crisis; and Job's inward conflict is becoming more and more intense. In his next two speeches he says little, almost nothing, to his friends.

He merely in a few words at the beginning gives vent to his impatience at their unfeeling speeches and begs them to desist and torture him no longer. He makes no reply to their arguments, but turns from them to God and pours forth all the agitation of his soul before him. Despair and hope alternate in his bosom, and the struggle is a fearful one indeed.

His agony and inward distress are at their highest point, and are reflected in the vehemence and even passionate character of his expressions. He is bowed down by the sense of God's anger as apparently shown in these terrible inflictions:

He tears *me* in His wrath, and hates me;
He gnashes at me with His teeth . . .
I was at ease, but He has shattered me;
He also has taken *me* by my neck, and shaken me to pieces;
He has set me up for His target,
His archers surround me.
He pierces my heart and does not pity;
He pours out my gall on the ground.
He breaks me with wound upon wound;
He runs at me like a warrior . . .
My face is flushed from weeping,
And on my eyelids *is* the shadow of death (16:9, 12–14, 16).

And all this, as his inward consciousness of integrity and his total inability to comprehend why God should have treated him thus, prompt him to exclaim:

. . . no violence is in my hands,
And my prayer is pure (16:17).

Such violent treatment, which he has no consciousness of having deserved, dealing with him as though he were a gross offender, which he was not, and carrying the infliction even to the point of destroying his life, extorts from him the passionate outcry as from the victim of atrocious injury:

O earth, do not cover my blood,
And let my cry have no *resting* place! (16:18).

[83]

I must die, but it is unrighteous murder. Let the earth refuse to drink in my blood thus unjustly shed, so that it may remain forever exposed, a constant witness to the terrible wrong perpetrated upon me; and let my death-cry never be hushed to silence, but resound forever in testimony of the cruel violence under which I suffer. I die, unable longer to sustain these dreadful inflictions which God is bringing upon me; but I die, protesting against the injustice and the outrage.

Has Satan then gained his end and has Job at length fallen into the snare? In the frightened darkness which has, to outward view, obscured the evidence of God's rectitude, has Job given up his sense of that rectitude? Is his confidence in God's eternal justice gone? Then has he indeed been driven to that renunciation of God's service to which Satan has been relentlessly endeavouring to force him?

But no! In all this agony and darkness and inexplicable mystery, Job cannot let go his ineradicable trust in God. Brought, as it might seem that he was, almost to the point of abandoning it, the strength of that trust only becomes more conspicuous from the strain to which it has been subjected. By its powerful recoil it carries him suddenly back from the verge of the abyss to the immovable foundation.

The faith that seemed to be vanishing, if it had not already vanished, rises unexpectedly superior over all the tumult of his soul and all depressing circumstances. From his frantic outcry against the injustice that is slaying him, he passes to the instant expression of his unabated trust in God.

> Surely even now my witness *is* in heaven,
> And my evidence is on high.
> My friends scorn me;
> My eyes pour out *tears* to God (16:19–20).

It is only the infinite exaltation of the Most High that, interposing an impassable obstruction, places him at such a remove that his case cannot be adequately brought before God to be rectified. And yet he pleads with God, who alone will or can, to be his surety and take his part. All others have deserted him. All others misunderstand his character and misinterpret his condition. God is his only refuge. But, under the returning sense of his misery and approaching end, he sinks once more at the close of his speech into a cheerless and despondent frame.

But the victory for which he has been struggling is now near at hand. The elements of hope, which have been gathering in his soul, have attained a consistency, which will make them superior in the strife. And his trust in God is preparing to assert itself invincibly, though deprived of all external supports and in the face of all opposition from outward sense.

The more particular examination of the language of his triumph will occupy another chapter. But to him who kept Job from stumbling, and who is able likewise to keep us from stumbling, and to present us faultless before the presence of his glory with exceeding joy, to God our Saviour, who alone is wise, be glory and majesty, dominion and power, both now and forever. Amen (*Jude* 24–25).

7

Job's Triumph

For I know that my Redeemer lives, and he shall stand at last on the earth; and after my skin is destroyed, this I know, that in my flesh I shall see God, whom I shall see for myself, and my eyes shall behold, and not another. How my heart yearns within me! (Job 19:25–27).

Job's triumphant assertion of his unshaken confidence in God, which he reaches near the close of the nineteenth chapter, is deservedly ranked as the most important passage in all his discourses. In some respects it is one of the most signal passages in the entire Old Testament, not so much in the positive amount of revelation which it contains as in the intrepid spirit of an unconquerable piety which it discloses. It exalts the patriarch of Uz to a level with the patriarch of Ur, the acknowledged father of the faithful, and marks Job as no less conspicuously an example and a pattern of faith than Abraham – the one as distinguished and heroic in his constancy in suffering as the other in his unswerving obedience.

The central position of this noble utterance in the discourses of Job has already been referred to. It is the turning-point in his discussions with his friends, the culmination and the close of his sore inward conflict, the full and complete expression of a trust which has been gradually gathering strength in the face of the most formidable opposition, and struggling to find expression, and it is the crowning victory over Satan's fiercest and most subtle temptation. It is faith planting itself firmly on the unseen when not one single external ground of support remains. The flukes of his anchor have taken hold of the immovable Rock of Ages, and the rage of the tempest and the dashing waves and the heaving sea cannot tear his vessel from its moorings.

Held by the strong grasp of the invisible, which is no less real, solid, and abiding because it is out of sight, he can safely defy all that is visible and on the surface, the mutable and the transient; and Satan's most furious assaults have no power to dislodge him or unsettle his sure well-grounded persuasion.

The suffering patriarch is, to all human appearance and in his own estimation, sinking rapidly to the grave under an accumulation of disasters which seem to exhaust Satan's fiendish ingenuity of torture and which appear to portend the divine displeasure. His friends asssure him that God is in this bearing testimony against his aggravated criminality.

Conscious of his integrity, yet confounded by these apparent evidences of God's hostility to him, he piteously pleads with God no longer to treat him as a criminal, since he does not deserve to be so treated, but to remove his heavy hand and openly bear witness to his innocence and uprightness.

But his cries are unanswered. He cannot get his case before the supreme Judge of all so as to obtain the hearing and the adjudication to which he makes his ineffectual appeal. The Most High does not in any way interfere to take his part, or to redress the wrongs which his servant is enduring, or to correct the grievous and unjust imputations which offer themselves as so direct an inference from God's own dealings with him. The heavens are silent. The situation remains unchanged. The sufferings of Job are unabated. His friends continue to taunt him with this plain evidence of guilt.

We have observed the growing intensity of Job's inward struggle and the strife is not yet allayed. He repels the insinuations of his friends. He rejects their conclusion, for it is contradicted by his own consciousness; but he cannot break the logic of their argument. As a consequence he is tossed by conflicting emotions.

He seems to be shut up to the conclusion that God is unrighteously oppressing him, afflicting him without cause or punishing him for crimes which he has not committed. And if God be unrighteous, he is not a God to be worshipped and confided in. If he admit this, he has fallen before the temptation, and Satan has gained his end. But how can he escape it? The facts stare him sternly in the face. And even if he were disposed to shut his eyes to them, his friends with officious pertinacity are for ever obtruding them upon him with their inevitable deductions.

It is a time of outspoken frankness, in which the convictions of his soul utter themselves without reserve and without disguise. He cannot shelter himself behind conventional phrases which, though they may have a religious sound, are emptied of their meaning and not expressive of his real and honest faith. He is not in a mood to save appearances by the gloss of pious professions. He dares not deceive himself and others even by uncandidly smoothing over difficulties in the divine administration, and persuading himself that he has explained what he has simply evaded.

His whole soul is opened before us down to its inmost depths and his most secret imaginings. He is engaged in a contest for life or death, in which everything is involved and no mere pretence or flimsy material can avail him. He must have truth, the solid basis of truth on which he can rest and will not lay claim to a piety based on shallow pretext or insincere profession.

In the unshrinking truthfulness with which he utters his inmost feelings, we are startled sometimes by the boldness and seeming irreverence with which he arraigns the rectitude of the divine proceedings. But it is not the daring recklessness of presumptuous speculation intruding on the unrevealed; nor is it the profane utterance of the impious transgressor blaspheming his Maker. It is the transparent sincerity of the tempted soul, driven almost to distraction by suggestions which are forced upon him, and which he cannot shut out. They are not cherished thoughts on which he loves to dwell and to which he gladly reverts. They are like frightful spectral illusions from which he shrinks away, but which continue nevertheless to glare upon him until, by the surpassing energy of faith, the dreadful spell is broken, and the temptation vanquished.

In his former speeches Job has been struggling desperately with the idea perpetually thrust upon him by his friends, and forcing itself upon him from all that he endured, that God was his enemy. Germs of hope have arisen within him but they have not been sufficient to lift the burden off his heart.

In the beginning of this speech he is still oppressed by these evident tokens of God's antagonism. But the argument of guilt deduced from it by his friends, he warmly repels. It is not true, as they urge, that he deserves what he suffers. It is not true that this is a display of divine justice: no, it is injustice:

> If indeed you exalt *yourselves* against me,
> And plead my disgrace against me,
> Know then that God has wronged me,
> And has surrounded me with His net (19:5–6).

Literally, God has perverted, distorted, and wronged me. It is the very word that Bildad had used in a former address, in his pious indignation at the sentiments of Job:

> Does God subvert judgment?
> Or does the Almighty pervert justice? (8:3).

And it is the same that Elihu uses subsequently in his rebuke of Job's rash and impatient utterances:

> Surely God will never do wickedly,
> Nor will the Almighty pervert justice (34:12).

[89]

But such perversion Job boldly affirms to exist in his own case. In his conscious integrity he denies the righteousness of any infliction which charges that upon him of which he is not guilty; he denies the justice of executing sentence upon him for crimes of which he was free. If God, in sending these sufferings upon him, has marked him out as a criminal, as his friends allege, then he has perverted justice, he has done him wrong. He adds:

If I cry out concerning wrong, I am not heard.
If I cry aloud, *there is* no justice (19:7).

He is the innocent victim of most cruel treatment. He is the defenceless subject of ruffian-like violence, who screams for help against pitiless and inhuman outrage, who calls for justice against the most grievous oppression and wrong. But his cries are uttered in vain. No help is afforded him and there is no relaxation of the extreme of injury inflicted. And he proceeds with his harrowing recital of these causeless and gratuitous inflictions:

He has fenced up my way, so that I cannot pass;
And He has set darkness in my paths.
He has stripped me of my glory,
And taken the crown *from* my head.
He breaks me down on every side,
And I am gone;
My hope he has uprooted like a tree.
He has also kindled His wrath against me,
And he counts me as one of his enemies.
His troops come together
And build up their road against me;
They encamp all around my tent (19:8–12).

My brethren, acquaintances, kinsfolk, familiar friends, my servants, maids, my very wife – all whom I loved are turned against me.

My bone clings to my skin and to my flesh,
And I have escaped by the skin of my teeth.
Have pity on me, have pity on me, O you my friends,

For the hand of God has struck me!
Why do you persecute me as God *does*,
And are not satisfied with my flesh? (19:20–22).

Why will you too join in this relentless persecution which
God has initiated against me, and which can only be compared to ravenous and savage beasts of prey tearing and
gnawing my flesh with insatiate greediness?

Against such cruelty and injustice on the part both of God
and man he enters his earnest protest and he would have his
words put on permanent record. Outcast alike from God and
man, he makes his appeal to the rocks. Let the enduring rock
be his monumental witness. Let there be carved there, in
letters that shall not fade, the inscription of his innocence.

Though God and man combine to condemn him, let his
own asseverations of his integrity be graven with an iron pen,
and be filled in with lead in the rock forever. And thus may
the everlasting rocks, in legible inscriptions never to be
effaced, bear testimony on his behalf; and may the justice that
he vainly craves elsewhere find at least its indelible and faithful record there.

It is customary to understand Job here as saying that he
would have the words which immediately follow graven in
the rock. He would have that golden sentence, 'I know that
my Redeemer lives . . .' (19:25) stand on perpetual record, his
legacy to future ages, his testimony through all time that, forsaken as he seemed to be by God and man, he never gave up
his confident trust in God his Saviour.

In his last and darkest hours he still held fast his unwavering assurance that God was his Redeemer and friend, and
though his body perished and crumbled into dust, he would
still with his own eyes see God who would appear on his
behalf. And if any prefer so to interpret the patriarch's wish,
we make no serious objection.

These words are certainly worthy of being recorded on
the solid rock. No grander monumental inscription can be
found. Job could not have a worthier epitaph upon his

rock-hewn tomb. In no way could a more exalted testimony be rendered to his steadfast piety than by preserving this outburst of triumphant faith, uttered under such circumstances. These words stand out conspicuously upon the speeches of Job as the noblest, the loftiest, the most characteristic that he ever uttered, and the most aptly significant of the power of his faith and the reality of his pious trust in God. So that, as has been said before, if any prefer to regard these as the words which Job would have to be carved upon the rock, we make no serious objection.

Yet it seems to us that those interpreters have more accurately divined Job's own meaning who think that he would have in lasting record on the rock not the particular statement about to be made, but the asseverations and protestations of his innocence to which he had given utterance over and over again in this and former speeches. So that this desire to have his words inscribed upon the rock is not so much an introduction to what follows, anticipating and preparing for the exultant announcement he is about to make, as rather the conclusion of what precedes.

It represents not his rising consciousness of triumph, but rather his lowest depth of desolation and hopeless despair, joined with his inward consciousness of integrity that demands some recognition. Bereft of every helper, human and divine, crushed beneath an unrighteous sentence, his appeals to God unheard, and his friends joining in the merciless persecution, he asks that the rocks may take up his dying declaration, and that his words may be indelibly written there, so that the imperishable stone may speak his innocence of these false charges, and testify of the wrong that has been done him, after his own voice is hushed.

And thus his appeal to the rocks to transmit his defence to all coming time will be parallel to his passionate apostrophe to the earth in his last preceding speech:

O earth, do not cover my blood,
And let my cry have no *resting* place! (16:18).

It is the outcry of one hopelessly overwhelmed by unjust imputations and wrongful treatment, but to whom his integrity is dearer than his life, and who insists that what is true and right shall have the assertion to which it is entitled; and who cannot but believe after all that eternal justice shall find a response somewhere and at some time.

This view of these words is confirmed by the form of Job's triumphant declaration which follows. This is not a separate, disconnected sentence, as though it were framed to be inscribed by itself upon the rock; but it is intimately linked with what precedes, as though it had been intended not to stand alone, but to form part of a continuous context, beginning as it does with a conjunction. 'For I know', or, more exactly rendered, 'And I know that my Redeemer lives' (19:25). A monumental inscription could not begin with 'And'. This necessarily marks a connection with some thought either expressed or implied in what precedes. And this connection or continuation, while it would be wholly wanting in an isolated record on the rocks, is readily traceable upon the explanation adopted above.

Perishing under groundless accusations of whose falsity he is profoundly conscious, but which he has no means of adequately refuting; God apparently testifying against him by the sufferings which he sends; his friends open-mouthed and loud in their reproaches and censures; deserted by all, and despairing of relief from any quarter, he utters as his last wish, while the grave is opening before him, that this amount of justice may be done him, to place his asseveration of innocence on record in the rock.

And as he utters the wish, the certainty that justice must and will be done flashes with strong conviction on his soul. I have asked a record on the rock; and all the while I know that my Redeemer lives. I need no monument of stone to vindicate me, no inscription graven with an iron pen and filled in with letters of molten lead. I have an ever-living and almighty Redeemer, who will rescue me from wrong, and defend me against calumny, and who will certainly, and in spite of all present appearances, reveal himself to me as my friend, and to whom, therefore, with implicit confidence, I entrust my cause.

Who the Redeemer is in whom Job thus affirms his confidence cannot admit of a moment's doubt. It is the same of whom he had declared in his preceding speech, 16:19,

> Surely even now my witness *is* in heaven,
> And my evidence is on high,

whom he had supplicated to be his pledge (17:3) when all others refused to espouse his cause; and of whose sentence in his favour he had again and again expressed his strong assurance, if his cause could but be brought before him so as to obtain his decision. Now all doubts have vanished: every condition that had previously clogged his hopes is removed. The LORD has undertaken for him. The LORD has engaged upon his side. The LORD will defend him against all injury and wrong. God, who seems to be persecuting him with such relentless hostility, is not his enemy; he is his Redeemer.

It is commonly supposed, and with reason, that in this word 'redeemer' there lies an allusion to an institution dating from the simple and as yet but partially regulated society of patriarchal times, and which was subsequently admitted with some restrictions and modifications into the Mosaic code. It was the office of the next of kin to espouse the cause of his injured or impoverished relative; to redeem his property, and restore it to him if he had in any way forfeited it or been obliged to sell it; to defend him against injury and wrong; and, especially, to avenge his blood if he had been unrighteously slain.

Now God has assumed the part of the next kinsman in relation to Job. He shall redress his wrongs; he shall avenge his injuries; he shall deliver him out of the bondage of his sorrows – the very figure which is employed in a subsequent part of this book, where the LORD is said to have 'turned the captivity of Job'. The frequency with which the title of Redeemer is applied to God in the Old Testament makes still plainer its application here. Jacob speaks of the divine angel that redeemed him from all evil (*Gen.* 48:16). Moses sings:

> You in Your mercy have led forth
> The people whom You have redeemed (*Exod.* 15:13).

David invokes the Lord, his strength and his Redeemer (*Psa.*19:14). With Isaiah it is a favourite name: The Redeemer the Lord of hosts, who is First and who is Last (*Isa.* 44:6).

When Job expresses his assurance that his Redeemer *lives,* he means not merely that he now exists, as opposed to the idea that there is no one now existing who can appreciate his case and understand his real character, and who was willing to avow himself his friend, nor that it is not until some future generation in a distant age shall read with unprejudiced eye his words sculptured in the rock that he can have an advocate or friend. Nor is it simply meant that he possesses a conscious existence in contrast with the lifeless, insensate rock; so that Job is not limited to the mute testimony carved upon the motionless, unconscious stone.

He has a *living* witness and defender. Nor is it simply existence in its highest style that is here affirmed, as though he claimed that his Redeemer was the ever-living one, to whom life is essential and inherent, the self-existent and eternal. But life involves active agency in the character maintained, or in the sphere to which it belongs; as when the Lord is styled the living God in contrast with dead and lifeless idols, who are of no service to their worshippers, who 'cannot do evil, nor can they do any good' (*Jer.* 10:5).

The *living* God is a God who has power to save and to destroy, and who exerts his power as the occasion demands. A *living* Redeemer is one who is more than a nullity or a name: He is one who will act as such, and act with real, substantial effect.

The rest of Job's triumphant testimony, as it appears in the Authorized Version, would lead us to suppose that Job expected his vindication to be postponed until the end of the world and the general resurrection. It runs thus: 'For I know *that* my Redeemer liveth, and *that* he shall stand at the latter *day* upon the earth; and though after my skin *worms* destroy this *body*, yet in my flesh I shall see God' (19:25). The translators have here followed older versions; and, without designing to warp the meaning of Job or to change the purport of his words, they have been unconsciously guided in the sense which they have assigned to his expressions by their knowledge of doctrines subsequently revealed with a clearness greater than that with which they had been made known in the time of Job, or with which they are here presented to his own mind.

Job is speaking under strong excitement, and in the language of lofty poetry. He uses no superfluous words. He simply indicates his meaning in the most concise manner, without rounding out his periods or using those connectives and significant particles which would be demanded in perspicuous prose. Hence his sentences are abrupt and elliptical and exactness of translation is difficult.

The embarrassment of the English translators is shown by the unusual number of italicized words, and these of no small importance to the meaning, which are heaped together in these verses. There are a few grammatical questions in the original passage which it is difficult to settle with absolute certainty, but which, however determined, do not materially affect the general sense. Without laying any stress upon these, therefore, we propose the following rendering as sufficiently accurate for our present purpose: 'And I know my Redeemer liveth, and last on earth shall He arise; and after my skin, which has been destroyed thus, and out of my flesh shall I see God.'

He says not that his Redeemer shall stand upon the earth or make his appearance upon it, but that he shall arise, address himself to action. He shall no longer sit still, as though he were not concerned or were disposed to take no part in what was transacting. He shall arise and participate actively in the matter. As when the suffering psalmists so often call upon God to arise:

Arise, O LORD;
Save me, O my God! (*Psa.* 3:7).

Arise, O LORD;
Do not let man prevail (*Psa.* 9:19).

Arise for our help,
And redeem us for Your mercies' sake (*Psa.* 44:26).

My Redeemer shall arise last; which may mean simply, he shall arise at last or hereafter. Or the strict force of the words may be retained. Job and his friends had been contending first. He shall arise last, enter latest on the scene, with the implication that he shall take the matter entirely into his own hands, and settle it unresisted in his own way. And still further, for this too lies in the proper meaning of the word, this shall be the final settlement of this much disputed case. He is the last, and none shall come after him to derange or alter what he has done. It is a word that looks to all futurity, and stretches to the utmost limit of time even reaching out to a boundless eternity; for it is the term applied to the unending duration of God himself, who is the First and who is the Last.

He shall arise last on earth, here spoken of as the scene of the conflict and the trials which he is to terminate and rectify. Or, as the words may mean, and some able interpreters with a measure of plausibility understand them to mean, 'over the dust'; the dust, that is, into which my body has meanwhile mouldered away. Upon which rendering there would here be a distinct assertion of what was already, perhaps, involved in the term 'last', and what is more fully brought out in the words that follow, that this intervention of his great Redeemer shall occur after he is dead. It will not take place until his body shall have been committed to the grave, and mouldered back to dust.

But whether this meaning be expressed in this particular phrase or no, it is made distinctly prominent in what follows: 'And after my skin which has been destroyed thus, and out of my flesh I shall see God.' He looks to a period after the destruction, the complete disintegration of his skin; and when he himself, the living part, the vital spirit, shall be separated from his flesh, his decaying and lifeless body. The just sense of these expressions compels us to regard Job as contemplating the time after he shall be dead, and affirming that then his Redeemer God shall manifest himself to his disembodied spirit.

Another interpretation which has been put upon this verse, and upon this whole passage, conceives Job to be here looking forward not to a future state, but to the restoration of God's favour, and his own deliverance out of all his troubles in the present life. This is not wholly a modern view, nor has it been confined to unbelieving interpreters. On the contrary, it was adopted by some of the most eminent of the Christian Fathers; and it has been ably advocated both in ancient and in recent times. The decisive objections to it are:

1. It does not give their fair meaning to the expressions just recited, which must denote something more than a skin damaged, and a body emaciated by disease. It is something subsequent to the total destruction and dissolution of the body that is referred to.

2. This is further evident from the constant tenor of Job's language elsewhere. He regards himself as on the verge of the grave, which is already claiming him as its own (17:1). Every earthly hope is annulled. Every temporal prospect has vanished. He invariably repels the idea, whenever his friends present it to him, of any improvement of his condition in this world as plainly impossible, and as though the very suggestion of it were an insult to his understanding. He cannot, therefore, himself anticipate what he uniformly pronounces irrational and absurd.

3. The same thing appears from the general drift of his argument with his friends, both prior to this passage and subsequent to it. His friends affirm that men are rewarded or punished in this life according to their characters. Job steadfastly denies it. If he here utters his expectation that God will

interfere to reward his piety in the present life, he completely abandons his own position, and adopts theirs.

4. His desire to have his protestation of his innocence recorded in ineffaceable characters upon the rock becomes ridiculous, if he cherished the assurance that the strife between him and his friends would be settled in his favour by a divine intervention in his own lifetime.

5. This passage forms the grand climax in the utterances of Job's faith and pious trust, to which he has from the first been slowly but steadily rising. He has voiced before the hypothesis of a life beyond the grave, though under the impossible condition of a return to this earthly life from the silence and the darkness of the tomb, when God's favour should be restored to him once more, and he should again have a desire and a loving regard for the work of his own hands. In another passage he had uttered his outcry of atrocious murder, and appealed to the earth not to cover his blood unjustly shed, and he had found the witness to his integrity in heaven.

He now takes one step in advance and faith reaches its clearest and fullest expression and confident assurance takes the place of a fitful, trembling hope. The hypothetical life beyond the grave becomes a real vision of God by his disembodied spirit. The witness to his integrity on high, to whom he had appealed to become his surety, but without any positive response, becomes his Redeemer, the avenger of his innocent blood, vindicating him, appearing as his champion, and on his behalf, and, as he in the next following verses warns his friends, punishing them that have done him wrong.

6. It very materially lowers the evidence and the power of Job's faith if we suppose him to be referring to the present life. The victory which he here gains, and which assures his triumph over Satan's temptation – over every possible temptation, in fact – is the victory of faith over outward sense. If any possible hope were left him in this world, the triumph would be less conspicuous and complete. It is only when we

see him shut up absolutely to the unseen, and perceive that with his trust in God he ventures boldly into it, not groping blindly or bewildered as in the dark, nor hesitating as in uncertainty or perplexity, nor shrinking as from possible danger or mistake, but confident as if treading on solid ground, and amid positive and ascertained realities, that we discern the true heroism of a faith like that of Job, and its unconquerable energy.

In his own esteem he is sinking into the grave with every indication surrounding him of God's relentless hostility; every possibility of a return of God's favour to him in this life is, to his mind, utterly shut out; and yet so fixed is he in his inward persuasion of the real friendship and redeeming grace of God to him, that he bursts the boundaries of time, passes the limits of the visible and the tangible, and knows that the manifest tokens of the divine love, which are denied him here, will be granted to him there. What can shake the trust or destroy the peace of that man who rests his certain hope on the immutable attributes of God? Satan and the world may vent their rage and ply their arts against him in vain. He is proof against every assault; for his steadfast trust is founded upon the eternal rock, and this is a foundation which never can be shaken.

It is no real objection to the view which has been taken of this passage, that in the subsequent course of the history God actually did interfere for the delivery of his servant and the restoration of his prosperity in the present life. What was in the secret purpose and plan of God must be carefully distinguished from Job's situation as it appeared to his own mind. It was the fact of his being left so entirely in the dark, and without the slightest clue afforded him respecting the design or issue of his sufferings, that created all the mystery of the dispensation, and laid such demands upon his faith, and established such a searching test of the reality and strength of his piety and adherence to God's service. God did indeed remove Job's sorrows, and renewedly grant him the open pledges of his favour in this life. He thus rewarded his servant's faith, contrary to and beyond all expectation. Job never dreamed of such a result, as all his speeches show, nor once conceived it possible.

Nor is there any force in the objection that Job has in his previous speeches uniformly spoken of death as the end of every activity and hope and has never let fall a syllable from which it could be inferred that he believed in the reality and certainty of a future state. The conclusion has hence been drawn that this cannot have been an article of his faith, and that he could not therefore have referred to it in the passage now under consideration.

But this is to overlook entirely the progress in Job's own mind, which is delineated in such a vigorous and masterly manner in the course of his speeches. We see Job in the beginning involved in all the mist and obscurity which overhung the future state in the patriarchal age, when no clear and unambiguous revelations had been made upon this subject. The continued conscious existence of the soul was known, but all was vague and shadowy in regard to that other life. Job is, by the intensity of the struggle in which he was engaged, driven step by step into clearer views of this subject than he possessed before.

We can watch his gradual advances toward it, his uncertain reachings out after it. And here we see him grasping it with all the fulness of assured conviction, as the only way out of inextricable darkness and despair, the inevitable deduction of a most indubitable axiom, the only resting place of his unwavering trust in the immutable grace of God, which nothing can wrest from him. Of God's unchanging favour he is inwardly and most thoroughly persuaded. There is no room remaining for that favour to display itself to him in this world. And the imperative necessity of his holiest and firmest convictions compels him to the declaration, I know that God will manifest his favour to me, though it be after my body has decayed and my spirit has forsaken this tenement of clay.

Nor is there any greater weight in the additional objection that Job makes no further use of this great truth in his controversy with his friends. He never refers to it subsequently, whether to console himself under the rigours of his own hard lot, or to shed light upon the enigmas of Providence in the unequal distribution of good and evil, or to refute the constantly repeated tenet of his friends of a retribution in the present life. A doctrine of such vast importance in its bearings on the subject under discussion could not, it is alleged, flash up in one single passage, and then never be alluded to again. The fact that it is not brought up and insisted upon elsewhere, is held to warrant the inference that it is not really contained here.

But this is to mistake entirely the part which this doctrine plays in the book of Job. It is not offered as a solution of the enigmas of divine providence. It is not even presented as the basis of consolation for the tempted and afflicted. The comfort of the sorrowing rests on a deeper ground than this, as is subsequently unfolded in the speech of Elihu, and by the Lord himself, to whom it is reserved to present in its true light a subject which has only been growing more and more perplexed under the reasonings and discussions of Job and his three friends.

The doctrine of immortality comes in solely to still Job's inward conflict, and bring him to a settled conviction that there is peace between his soul and God, which no outward and temporal troubles can destroy. This it effectually does. Job's inward agitation ceases from this moment. He is no longer distracted by the sense of God's hostility and wrath. His outward situation is unchanged and the problem of his sufferings is as mysterious as ever; but he has attained to inward peace. He knows that his Redeemer lives, and that, after his worn and suffering body shall be resolved into dust, the clouds shall break away, which now obstruct his vision of the face of God. The lesson of immortality has accomplished its end. It need not, therefore, be repeated. And that it is not applied to matters with which, in the plan and purpose of this book, it has nothing to do, is surely no argument against its appearance here, where its introduction was essential.

But in what relation, it may be further asked, does this passage stand to the doctrine of the Messiah and of a corporeal resurrection? Is Job's Redeemer ours, and his faith the same in which the people of God now rejoice in the completed victory over death and the grave? In germ and substance it was, but, as it lay before his consciousness, not in the same developed form. God was his Redeemer: Christ, who was in the beginning with God and was God, is ours. When Job appeals to his Redeemer, he does so without even remotely apprehending that he is the second person of the Godhead; for of the distinction of persons in the divine Being, and of the doctrine of the Trinity as unfolded in the New Testament, he knew nothing. But he addresses him in a character and solicits the fulfilment of an office which distinctively belongs to God the Son.

He is, and has been in every age, the Redeemer out of every distress, the Guardian and Protector of his people, and their Deliverer both from temporal distress and from that everlasting woe of which the former is the figure and the type. It is he to whom the saints of God are indebted for that joyful prospect of the vision of God beyond the grave, to which Job looked forward. So that the doctrine of Christ is here approached from its divine side, not as the son of Abraham, but as the Son of God.

And then perhaps it may not be without its deeper significance and its divinely intended meaning that the term 'Redeemer' had the association linked with it, both in patriarchal and Mosaic usage, of the next of kin. Is there not here possibly a shadowing forth of more than Job himself intended or imagined when he used the word? An index pointing to that divine Redeemer, who is in everything our nearest kinsman, and who allied himself to us in the bonds of our common humanity, bone of our bone, and flesh of our flesh, that he might have a kinsman's right to espouse our cause, to vindicate us from the accusations of the law, and free us from the sentence of death written in our members, and open to us life and immortality with the beatific vision of

God? So that as Abraham saw Christ's day, it may likewise be said of Job that he rejoiced to see Christ's day, and he saw it and was glad. Only it was the seed of Abraham to whom the father of the faithful looked forward. It was his divine Redeemer who gladdened the believing soul of the man of Uz.

The human aspect of Christ's work, so far as it is foreshown in the book of Job, is chiefly set forth by Job himself, in his own person, as the type of the man of sorrows, forsaken and persecuted by his friends, and abandoned apparently by God, and yet for whom the cross was the passage way to the crown, and suffering to a glorious reward, and the fruit of the travail of whose soul abounded to the blessing of others, as Job's intercession brought healing to his three friends, and he has been a helper to the distressed from his own day to this.

The resurrection of the body was probably not present to Job's thoughts, certainly not in the form of a general and simultaneous rising from the dead. And yet it is so linked, seminally at least, with our continued spiritual existence, and it is so natural and even necessary for us to transfer our ideas of being, drawn from the present state, to the great hereafter, that it may perhaps be truly said that the germs of the doctrine of the resurrection may likewise be detected here:

Whom I shall see for myself,
And my eyes shall behold, and not another (19:27),

so natural was it to transfer the thought of these corporeal organs along with this personal identity, upon which he insists, even while speaking of himself as disembodied.

We shall not here revive the curious and profitless speculations to which these words have given rise, nor shall we involve ourselves in any discussion as to whether Job means the eyes of the soul or the eyes of the body. It is enough that we find here suggested the intimacy of the link which binds the two parts of our nature together, and the powerful association which almost inevitably carries us forward from the continued life of the soul to the restored life of the body.

And then, when we add to this the ambiguity of certain expressions here employed, and which may not have been wholly unintended (shall we say?) by the Spirit of truth, so that they yield themselves readily to the setting forth of the doctrine of the resurrection, as shown in the Authorized Version and in various other versions, ancient and modern, it will appear that this passage has not been without important bearings, at least, upon the history of the belief in this great and cardinal doctrine of the gospel of the Son of God, if not upon its actual disclosure in the course of divine revelation.

8

Job Refutes His Friends

How then can you comfort me with empty words, since falsehood remains in your answers? (Job 21:34).

The crisis of the temptation is past, but Job's perplexity is not yet removed. He refuses to be driven from his constant trust in God by all the influences that Satan has arrayed against him. Amidst all the seeming evidences of God's hostility, he maintains his confidence in him as his Redeemer. He who is afflicting him now will effect his deliverance hereafter. But the time of this deliverance has not yet come. He is walking in darkness, trusting in the LORD. The storm of calamity continues without abatement, and the mystery of his sorrows is still unsolved.

So far Job has spoken principally to God. It was with him that he had to do, rather than with his friends. What has been chiefly agitating him, and what was in fact the mainspring of the temptation, was the question of his personal relation to his Maker. When his friends affirmed and reiterated, as they did in every speech they made, the doctrine of a providential retribution, that it was the wicked who suffered under God's righteous rule and in proportion to their wickedness, Job made immediate application of this, as they designed that he should, to his own case. He had, indeed, more than once declared the falsity of this general principle, saying:

> Therefore I say, 'He destroys the blameless and the wicked.'
> If the scourge slays suddenly,
> He laughs at the plight of the innocent.
> The earth is given into the hand of the wicked.
> He covers the faces of its judges (9:22–24).

> The tents of robbers prosper,
> And those who provoke God are secure—
> In what God provides by His hand (12:6).

But this was only incidental to the main current of his thoughts. He was in no mood for an abstract discussion. The personal question involved in it swallowed up every other consideration. It concerned what was dearer to him than life. It affected the very foundation of his trust in God. It was not simply that he had a tender regard for his reputation and that he could not bear to have a cloud brought over his good name.

He who had borne the loss of property and children, and endured the sufferings inflicted on his own person with such noble resignation, could also have submitted with equanimity to unjust censures and false reproaches. That was not, dear as his good name was to him, the tenderest and most vital point. The estimation in which he was held by his fellow-men was not his chief treasure.

But his conscious integrity was an inalienable possession. This he could not part with. And if the affirmation of his friends was true, and the rectitude of him who ruled the world seemed to give it sanction, then God was punishing him for crimes which he was conscious that he had never committed. He was, indeed, in a most pitiable dilemma. If he denied the position of his friends then the plain inference was that God was unjust. If he assented to it, then God was unjust. And, in either case, how could he serve a God who was not only unjust, but so pitiless and so cruel?

Satan seemed, at length, to have driven him into a position from which there was no escape. How can he do otherwise than renounce the service of God? What basis remains for that confidence and reverential homage which is essential to true worship? Satan has completely enveloped him with his deadly snare, and it would appear as though there were no alternative. Job must fall before his adversary.

We have traced the fierce and weary conflict to its final issue. We have watched him in his inward strife, in his piteous moans, his expostulations with God, his vain appeals to him to declare himself on his side. We have seen him driven to and fro in his tumultuous agitation, until, forced to the very edge of the precipice, and apparently about to fall hopelessly and helplessly into the awful chasm that yawned beneath him, he cleared it by one energetic act of faith, reaching forth into the unseen, and sustaining himself without any visible support.

The personal question is now settled, and his intense inward agitation has subsided. He is in a much calmer and more tranquil state of mind. He has gained that unshaken conviction of the rectitude and goodness of God which enables him to claim him as his Redeemer in spite of all adverse appearances. This source of his disquiet is put to rest. The power of the temptation is broken. Satan cannot detach him from the service of God, seeing that he holds fast to his faith in him, in spite of all the suggestions of sense and of reason.

Job is safe from falling. But outward sense and human reason still present a problem, which baffles him completely. He holds fast to his confidence in God, but he is bewildered nevertheless. The solution of his friends is no solution. According to their principles, indeed, there is no enigma in providence. They see nothing but the evident and uniform reign of justice. Job shows, on the contrary, that this is not the case. He takes issue with them in regard to their fundamental

principle, and exposes its falsity. It is not, as they allege, a fact
of uniform experience that the righteous are rewarded and
the wicked suffer. This is the point to which he addresses
himself in his remaining speeches.

It is, as he avers, a most distressing truth, one that fills him
with painful emotions at every contemplation of it, and at
which they might well stand aghast themselves. The administration of this world is not conducted on such evident
principles of equity as they have maintained. He says:

> Look at me and be astonished;
> Put *your* hand over *your* mouth.
> Even when I remember I am terrified,
> And trembling takes hold of my flesh' (21:5–6).

So far from just retribution overtaking the guilty, bad men
are often signally prospered:

> Why do the wicked live *and* become old,
> Yes, become mighty in power?
> Their descendants are established with them in their sight,
> And their offspring before their eyes.
> Their houses *are* safe from fear,
> Neither *is* the rod of God upon them.
> Their bull breeds without failure;
> Their cow calves without miscarriage.
> They send forth their little ones like a flock,
> And their children dance.
> They sing to the tambourine and harp,
> And rejoice to the sound of the flute.
> They spend their days in wealth,
> And in a moment go down to the grave (21:7–13).

Their merry, joyous prosperity continues to the very last.
Experiencing no reverses and no unusual calamity, with no
check upon their good fortune, and no term of suffering that
could be regarded as a penalty for their misdeeds, they go
down peacefully and quietly to the grave. Their life is filled
up with pleasure, and with every form of earthly good to its
very close. And the natural consequence follows. In their
arrogant and impious presumption they refuse all subjection

to the Most High and say to God,

> 'Depart from us,
> For we do not desire the knowledge of Your ways.
> Who is the Almighty, that we should serve Him?
> And what profit do we have if we pray to him?' (21:14–15).

Bildad had said, 'The light of the wicked indeed goes out' (18:5); and 'destruction is ready at his side' (18:12). Job, with such facts of experience in mind as he has just recited, asks in reply, 'How often is this the case?' It is by no means the invariable rule.

> How often is the lamp of the wicked put out?
> *How often* does their destruction come upon them,
> The sorrows *God* distributes in his anger?
> They are like straw before the wind,
> And like chaff that a storm carries away (21:17–18).

But, interpose the friends, the retribution is sure to come: it is only awhile delayed. 'God lays up one's iniquity for his children' (21:19; cf. 5:4; 18:19; 20:10). This, Job retorts, is no retribution at all in any proper sense:

> Let Him recompense him [the sinner himself,
>   in his own person] that he may know *it*.
> Let his eyes see his destruction,
> And let him drink of the wrath of the Almighty.
> For what does he care about his household after him,
> When the number of his months is cut in half? (21:19–21).

How is he affected by what happens to his children, after he is dead and gone? They were presuming to 'teach God knowledge', by thus prescribing a law for his government of the world, and therefore might justly fear that sentence with which he rewards the proud.

On the other hand, he alleges that in actual fact there was no discrimination exercised in the fortunes allotted to men. No reason could be assigned why some men never have trouble, and others never have any thing else.

> For you say,
> 'Where *is* the house of the prince?

And where *is* the tent,
The dwelling place of the wicked?' (21:28),

implying that they have disappeared, or that their ruins only remain as monuments of God's righteous vengeance. But this is not so.

Have you not asked those who travel the road?
And do you not know their signs?
For the wicked are reserved for the day of doom;
They shall be brought out on the day of wrath (21:29–30).

They are often screened from calamities that befall better men. And when they die, instead of being followed by execrations or regarded as malefactors, cut off by the just sentence of heaven, they are buried with every mark of distinction, attendant crowds doing honour to their memory and perpetuating their pernicious example.

Astounded by this audacious attack upon their stronghold, this flat denial of what they have all along been asserting as an incontrovertible axiom, and the foundation of their whole argument, the friends are obliged to modify materially their method of attack. Eliphaz, who speaks next, comes to the rescue of the principle by a furious onslaught upon Job himself. Their oft-repeated maxim itself, in its broad universality, cannot again be affirmed in the face of what has just been said. But he is more than ever convinced that it exposes the real secret of all Job's troubles.

Whether it can be established as a general rule or not, whether it is applicable to all other cases or not, it unquestionably holds true with regard to Job. Eliphaz therefore restricts himself no longer to covert insinuations or indirect suggestions, but makes positive and explicit charges of enormous wickedness, and assigns this as the undoubted reason of Job's terrible afflictions.

God could have no motive for dealing with Job otherwise than with impartial justice. He must have been guilty, therefore, of atrocious crimes, the righteous penalty for which he is now enduring.

The whole matter is thus brought to a simple issue. Is Job a gross transgressor, or is he not? The charge is open, and unambiguous. Job promptly takes up the challenge, and meets the charge with an equally explicit denial.

God has indeed hidden himself in the mystery of these inexplicable sorrows, which continue to press upon him with the same dire weight as before. He is withdrawn beyond the reach of outward sense. But concealed as he is from sight, impossible as it is to penetrate to his secret seat to urge his plea, and to obtain the removal of these distresses under which he now groans, Job yet makes to him his confident appeal:

> But He knows the way that I take;
> *When* he has tested me, I shall come forth as gold.
> My foot has held fast to his steps;
> I have kept his way and not turned aside.
> I have not departed from the commandment of His lips;
> I have treasured the words of His mouth
> More than my necessary *food* (23:10–12).

And, as he proceeds to say, the world is full of just such enigmas, of open wickedness that is suffered to go unpunished, and of grievous wrongs that are not redressed.

As the charges brought against Job are wholly destitute of proof, being mere inferences from a principle, which, as has now been shown, is not verified by the actual experience of the world, Bildad cannot again repeat them in the face of Job's solemn asseveration of his innocence and his appeal to the searcher of hearts. There is consequently nothing for him to do, if he would maintain the show of an argument, but to fall back upon the sinfulness inherent in human nature. No man can be pure in the sight of the infinite God.

This point had been made by Eliphaz at the very outset of the discussion, and it had been sufficiently answered long since. Bildad, sensible of the weakness of his position, makes no attempt to illustrate or enforce it, and, after a few feebly uttered sentences, relapses into silence. The friends withdraw discomfited from the contest.

Job cannot refrain from taunting them with the completeness of their failure in an argument which they have been conducting with so much pretension. He then seizes the opportunity to guard his language against misconception. In saying what he had done respecting the inequalities of divine providence, he had neither meant to reflect on the glorious nature of God, nor to deny the existence of moral retributions.

He accordingly affirms the exalted majesty of God in as lofty terms as his friends themselves could employ. And, while continuing to insist upon his own integrity, notwithstanding the afflictions sent upon him, he freely admits, and this in language as emphatic as their own, the reality of God's providential government, and that punishment does overtake the ungodly. Nevertheless there is a mystery enveloping the divine administration, which is quite impenetrable to the human understanding.

This thought of the impossibility of men's arriving, by their own unaided powers, at any comprehension of the divine plan in the administration of the universe, is illustrated with great beauty. An apt figure is taken from the art of mining. Men can discover the precious and the useful metals, though they are hidden deep underground. They will descend into the bowels of the earth, and push their shafts remote from the habitation of men; and, regardless of the obstructions that block their way, and of the gathering streams that hinder their progress, and of the obscurity which reigns in these dark abysses, they cut a passage through the rocks, and beneath the mountains, to the treasures which they are seeking.

But there is a far greater treasure which cannot be thus obtained; a treasure that gold nor silver cannot equal, and which vastly exceeds in worth the most valued of jewels and precious stones. No ingenuity of men, and no search, however prolonged or anxious, can ever discover it:

But where can wisdom be found?
And where *is* the place of understanding? . . .

It is hidden from the eyes of all living,
And concealed from the birds of the air (28:12, 21).

Even the world of the departed does not possess it: they have 'heard a report about it' (28:22), but they are not able to grasp it. There is but one being in the universe who does possess a perfect comprehension of God's grand plan, and that is he who adjusted all things with infinite precision, and who is guiding all to his own preordained results. And he who is infinite in knowledge has disclosed to man wherein for him true practical wisdom lies.

God understands its way,
And He knows its place.
For He looks to the ends of the earth,
And sees under the whole heavens,
To establish a weight for the wind,
And apportion the waters by measure.
When He made a law for the rain,
And a path for the thunderbolt,
Then He saw *wisdom* and declared it;
He prepared it, indeed, He searched it out.
And to man He said,
'Behold, the fear of the Lord, that is wisdom,
And to depart from evil is understanding (28:23–28).

The providence of God is not conducted upon such a palpable rule, and one so perfectly simple and susceptible of easy application, as the friends have maintained. The dealings of the infinite God are not regulated upon a principle so obvious as to be level with the humblest understanding. On the contrary, they are enveloped in the profoundest mystery. It is impossible to lift the veil which obscures his designs, or to penetrate the reasons which govern the divine proceedings.

This is not because there is no reason in them, and wild confusion reigns. The impossibility of discovering the divine order does not arise from the absence of any real order in the universe. The world is not under the dominion of chance, swinging at random to and fro, without an aim, without intelligent oversight, a ship without chart or compass or rudder, tossed by the waves and driven by the winds. Nor is it under the blind sway of inexorable fate. Nor has it been surrendered to the mere control of physical laws, working out their fixed and uniform sequences with a relentless disregard of anything but inherent material properties, which, with undeviating precision, pursue each their own affinities, but own no superintending control, and are subordinated to no high moral aims and to no end superior to themselves. Nor is the Ruler of the world a capricious tyrant, whose absolute power is directed by mere arbitrary will, but with no wise forethought, no well-considered and worthy purpose.

Infinite wisdom reigns throughout the universe. He who adjusted the physical forces of external nature with such admirable precision, who balanced their action with such delicate nicety that perfect equilibrium is maintained, and no derangement ensues in the onward movement of all this complicated machinery through successive ages – he who established and perpetuates this universal harmony in all material things, giving their weight to the winds and their measure to the waters, orders with equal wisdom the multitudinous affairs of men. There is a divine method. There is an infinite plan, and it is one that is worthy of the supreme intelligence; it bears throughout the stamp of consummate wisdom. But it is past finding out.

We cannot attain to a comprehension of it. We cannot see how its several parts cohere with each other, or how they consist with the perfections of him who designed it and who is conducting it. There is much that, to human view, seems to be at variance with a well-ordered administration. There is much that we cannot account for, much that we cannot understand.

There are many things in the management of the world that completely baffle every attempt to solve them. We cannot see why they are, nor why God permits them, nor how he can consistently permit them. With our limited understandings and our restricted range of observation, we cannot pretend to fathom the bottomless deep, nor measure what has no bound. We cannot, even by the most prolonged search or the most elaborate investigation, attain to a thorough understanding of God's infinite designs. Wisdom rules in all, a wisdom more valuable than gold, and above the price of rubies.

But the keenest insight and the most indefatigable application of the human faculties fail to discover it. The secret that resolves all mysteries, harmonizes all strifes, reconciles all contradictions, and reduces this seemingly inextricable confusion to perfect symmetry and order, is hidden in the infinite mind alone.

Man can never comprehend the absolute wisdom but the Most High has, in condescending mercy, revealed to him all that is necessary for his practical guidance. He may not presume to know how God governs the world, or what rules he prescribes for his own procedure; but he has been sufficiently taught how to direct his own conduct and to govern his own life.

He cannot solve the mysteries of providence; but he may, by taking heed to the lessons given him, solve what is of more immediate moment to him, namely all questions of personal duty. He cannot tell the end, which is subserved by every thing which God permits or brings to pass; but he need be in no doubt how to accomplish the true end of his own being and to secure his own highest welfare – 'the fear of the Lord, that is wisdom, and to depart from evil is understanding' (28:28).

Job here pauses, as he had done once before, for his friends to make reply, if they have anything further to say. Whether on account of his obstinate persistence in his own views they think that it will be of no use to argue further, or whether they begin themselves to suspect the unsoundness of their position, and to perceive that there is more of mystery in the case of their suffering friend than they had imagined, they at any rate say nothing. And Job proceeds to state at length the unsolved enigma of his sorrows. His friends have shed no light upon this distressing dispensation, and he can get none himself. He dwells upon his former happy condition, then recites the dismal reverse which he has experienced, and finally, in the most solemn manner, affirms his innocence of any crime which could account for his being treated thus.

The words of Job are here ended. He stands face to face with a mystery that is thus far wholly unexplained. He has no theory, and can imagine none upon which his present sorrows can be accounted for. His friends undertook to silence his complaint, but he has silenced them. He holds fast to his faith in God, but he does so notwithstanding troubled questionings of which he cannot rid himself that have arisen in his soul, and notwithstanding the presence of facts which he can neither escape nor explain away, and which seem to be in direct contradiction to the divine attributes. As he gloomily said (23:15–16):

> Therefore I am terrified at His presence;
> When I consider *this*, I am afraid of Him.
> For God made my heart weak,
> And the Almighty terrifies me.

Uneasy apprehensions mingle with his thoughts of God, which he is unable to still. There is an unrest in his soul, which he cannot compose. Satan has not been able to destroy him, but he has plunged him into darkness and distress, out of which he cannot find his way. His pious trust continues. He still confides in his Redeemer, who after his skin is destroyed, and his flesh has mouldered back to dust, will reveal himself to his disembodied spirit. But will God suffer his servant to go on in darkness to the end, bearing his heavy burden, and hoping against hope? Must Job die under the cloud?

9

Elihu

Then the wrath of Elihu, the son of Barachel the Buzite, of the family of Ram, was aroused against Job; his wrath was aroused because he justified himself rather than God. Also against his three friends his wrath was aroused, because they had found no answer, and yet had condemned Job (Job 32:2–3).

The three friends of Job cannot answer him, and yet it is plain that he ought to be answered. He has silenced his friends, and has shown that the principle which they have so confidently urged will not explain the mystery of God's dealings in general, nor solve the enigma of his own case. But he has not brought the question to any satisfactory issue, nor to one in which it can be properly left. The friends undertook to justify God's providential dealings: The failure of their argument apparently leaves the divine proceedings open to censure and without any adequate vindication. They aimed to show Job that he had no right to complain of the sufferings which God had sent upon him or permitted to befall him, and they were not successful in their endeavour.

Job has triumphantly maintained his ground in his controversy with his friends; and, in his victory over them, there is the danger of his entertaining the impression, and the impression being made on others, that he is likewise in the right in his controversy with the providence of God. This dangerous impression needs to be corrected, both for his own sake and for the sake of those to whose instruction his great trial, and the book that records it, was designed to contribute.

In the vehemence of his opposition to his friends, and in the intensity of his inward struggles, Job has been betrayed into expressions, which cannot be approved, in which he seems to arraign the equity of the divine administration. Great consideration is requisite in weighing these expressions and in estimating their real meaning. Allowance must be made for the circumstances in which they were uttered. Words wrung from him in the bitterness of his heart and in the tumult of his feelings under the terrible pressure of his sorrows and the exasperating treatment of his friends, are not to be regarded as though they had been spoken in calmer moments.

But if Job had gone no further astray than this, that in his desperation and intolerable distress he had occasionally let slip what he subsequently regretted, and what did not express his real state of mind, no correction might have been deemed necessary. The fact, however, is that Job was involved in an irreconcilable conflict with himself.

He was in a dilemma from which he could not by any skill or power of his own be extricated. His most intimate and ineradicable convictions were seemingly at hopeless variance. On the one side was the consciousness of his own integrity, which was dearer to him than his life, which he could not deny nor part with, and which he was prepared to assert at all hazards. He knew from the testimony of his own conscience that he was not a gross and wicked offender; and he made his confident appeal to the Searcher of hearts for the uprightness of his past life. But how, then, can he maintain his confidence in the justice and rectitude of God in his providential govern-ment? A God who lets the wicked triumph and who afflicts the just, how can he be a righteous and a holy God? Job cannot put these two things together, though he holds them both and will not abandon either. And yet, in the honest frankness of his soul, he does not and cannot shut his eyes to the fact that they do seem to him to clash. And, as in the guilelessness of his nature, he makes no concealment; what he feels, he says.

His controversy with God's providence is not limited, therefore, to a few passionate outbursts, which in moments of reflection he would gladly recall. But it is forced upon him by an inward necessity which he cannot escape. He has justified his own integrity against the suspicions and accusations of his friends. But how is the righteousness of God to be vindicated? This is the problem. His friends can throw no light upon it, and he is as much in the dark as they. He still holds indeed, with an unslackened grasp, his confidence in God's righteousness, and he will not let it go. In his struggle to retain this great essential truth he had fought his way through to that grand burst of triumphant trust in God, in which he utters his faith in the unseen without any misgivings, though it was flatly contradictory to outward appearance saying, 'I know that my Redeemer lives' (19:25).

He believes that divine rectitude now so mysteriously hidden, shall yet appear and, though it suffers him to perish in this world, it will vindicate him in the next. But even this noble utterance leaves the black clouds of the present undispersed. The righteousness of God shall shine forth radiantly hereafter, but why is it so strangely obscured now? This Job cannot answer; and, though his trust abides in God's ultimate justice, it is after all a trust in a God who has hidden himself.

A glimpse into one design, at least, of this infliction has been afforded to the readers of the book at the outset in what is there said of the agency of Satan in bringing it about. This arch-fiend plots the ruin of Job. Quite discrediting the reality of goodness, he lays a snare, which he boastingly affirms will be effectual in overthrowing this godly man, and bringing him to abjure the service of his Maker. The Lord permits the tempter to try his arts to the full; and the result is his complete discomfiture. Hardly beset as Job was, and driven to the most desperate straits, he nevertheless holds fast his trust in God, and succeeds in trampling the temptation under foot. And thus it is whenever the malice of evil spirits and the rage of wicked men are allowed to assail the saints of God with a view to the more complete exhibition of the reality and power of their pious fear. God's martyrs, suffering for their attachment to their blessed Lord, and adhering to him in spite of all that can be employed to turn them from their fidelity, illustrate the reality of godliness, and glorify God in the fires.

We see Satan's design in Job's distresses, and how conspicuously it was foiled. But what did the Lord intend by them? This has not yet been stated. Nevertheless, we cannot but conceive that he had a design of his own in permitting Satan to make this furious onset upon Job. This cannot have been to gratify Satan's spleen, with which the Lord had no sympathy; nor can it have been that God needed such a test to satisfy himself of the reality of Job's piety, which he knew as thoroughly before the trial as after it, and to which he had already borne unqualified testimony; nor can we suppose that God would have allowed such overwhelming distresses to befall his faithful servant, merely to convince Satan of the falsity of his unreasonable and malicious suggestion.

God must have had a purpose of his own in all this, and which did not terminate upon others, but directly affected Job himself. God would not have made of his servant a passive instrument for accomplishing something in which he himself and his own interests were wholly disregarded. He would not have made him suffer as a mere spectacle for others, when there was no end to be answered affecting himself. There must have been some end, which, so far as Job himself was concerned, would be an ample justification of the providence of God in permitting him to be treated as he was, and to suffer as he did.

Some inkling of the divine purpose may be already gathered from what has thus far taken place. We have already seen how triumphantly Job bore the severe and searching test applied to him. And we may be sure that the desperate struggle, through which he passed, has developed and strengthened his piety. Job has learned to maintain his faith under new and most difficult circumstances. He has risen to a loftier exercise of faith than ever before. With no external props and aids, and in the face of all the suggestions of outward sense, he was obliged to maintain himself by the simple putting forth of faith in the unseen. His faith could not but gather strength and clearness by the effort. That Job learned to say with such positiveness, 'I know that my Redeemer lives' (19:25), in spite of all that conspired to extinguish his hopes and quench his pious trust, was attended with a positive and decided spiritual gain. He was lifted thereby into a higher spiritual sphere.

Associated with, or growing out of, this new elevation and increase of Job's faith is the fresh enlargement of his spiritual perceptions, and his keener insight into religious truth. In groping eagerly about for something to lean upon, for something to support his soul in this time of his deep distress, he grasps the firm pillar of his immortality, and puts it into a connection previously unknown or unthought of with his present needs. A new element of truth is won in the struggle, a new ground for the tempted to stand upon, a wellspring of consolation to thirsty, fainting souls.

Still, though we may gather something by inference respecting the design of God in this mysterious and clouded providence, we feel the need of some authoritative disclosure of this design. We feel this need likewise and particularly for Job's sake, and for those who are to be instructed by his example, that the question raised between him and his friends should be set at rest, that the truth should be distinctly stated which they have both vainly tried to discover so that the antagonistic principles in Job's soul might be composed and that the divine rectitude which has seemed to be impugned hitherto might find a just and satisfactory vindication.

The solution of the perplexed problem is given partly by Elihu and partly by the LORD himself. Elihu, who here appears for the first time and whose descent is somewhat particularly described as well as his motive for speaking, first addresses Job in a series of chapters, pausing at intervals apparently for the sake of affording an opportunity for a reply, if Job was disposed to make any. Job, however, says nothing. Then the LORD speaks to Job out of the whirlwind and finally brings the whole matter to a termination by restoring Job to more than his former prosperity.

No portion of this book has proved more embarrassing than the discourse of Elihu, and in regard to none has there been a greater diversity of views. There has been a wide divergence of opinion from very early times as to the part which is assigned to him, or why he is introduced at all; in what relation the solution of the enigma afforded by him stands to that which is furnished by the LORD, or why two solutions are given instead of only one.

The perplexity is increased by the difficulty on the one hand of harmonizing what Elihu says with the lessons to be drawn from the discourse of the LORD, and on the other of discriminating in a clear and satisfactory manner between the sentiments propounded by Elihu and those which had been previously advanced by Job's three friends.

Many have concluded that the lessons taught by Elihu and the LORD are hopelessly at variance, while the doctrine of Elihu and the three friends is identical; and, consequently, that what he says contributes nothing toward the true and proper settlement of the question at issue. The solution which he offers of the enigmas of providence is alleged to be substantially that of Eliphaz and his associates, and accordingly open to the same condemnation, and to be regarded as set aside by the subsequent decision rendered by the LORD himself, which is alone to be accepted as the true solution, and the one which adequately meets the case. On this hypothesis Job does not reply to Elihu, because he really advances nothing new, and nothing which he had not sufficiently answered before. And the LORD makes no allusion to him, because he is a mere intruder who has said nothing deserving of special regard; and he is, moreover, involved in the censure passed upon the friends, whose tenets he had simply repeated.

Among those who hold this view there is still a diversity of judgement as to the ability displayed by Elihu in the presentation of his argument. In the opinion of some he is a shallow pretender, a vain and conceited upstart, intruding his weak opinions unsolicited, where wiser and better men had already exhausted that side of the question and spoken with more force than he is able to do. Others concede to his argument distinguished merit, and think that his several points are put with great skill and cogency.

They consider him the exponent of human reason, representing the highest results to which it is capable of attaining without an immediate divine revelation. He fails to give the true solution of the mysterious problems of divine providence, but he only does so because they are not within the grasp of man's unaided intellect. God can alone give the correct answer where the wisest and most sagacious of men are incompetent to discover the truth. The failure of Elihu to advance the settlement of the question beyond the point at which the friends had left it is thus supposed to render still more palpable the necessity for the LORD himself to intervene, if the matter is ever to be put upon its proper basis.

It seems highly improbable, however, that so much space would be devoted to a personage who really contributes nothing whatever to the design of the book, and only repeats what the friends had already substantially said before. This view, therefore, very naturally paved the way for another which has also had not a few advocates, that the speech of Elihu forms no part of the book as originally written, but is an addition by a later hand. This, as some think, mars the symmetry and completeness of the work, or, according to others, adds fresh and valuable thoughts, but such as did not enter into the plan of the original writer.

The difficulties which have been felt with regard to Elihu will, we are persuaded, disappear, and the hypotheses already referred to, which are built upon them, will vanish upon a more careful study of the speech attributed to him, and of the language with which he is introduced. It is plain that the writer of the book does not regard him as siding with the friends in their controversy with Job. He represents him as equally displeased with the positions of both the contending parties. 'Then the wrath of Elihu . . . was aroused against Job; his wrath was aroused because he justified himself rather than God. Also against his three friends his wrath was aroused, because they had found no answer, and yet had condemned Job' (32:2–3).

He accordingly steps forth as an arbiter, and puts the question at issue upon entirely new ground. He agrees, to be sure, with the friends in some of their positions, which as general statements were quite correct. But his fundamental tenet is totally different from theirs, as will be seen presently.

Elihu is not spoken of in the beginning of the book, when the arrival of the three friends is mentioned, because there was no occasion for speaking of him then. He only engages in the dispute because the three friends have failed to find a satisfactory answer to Job; and to refer to him in the outset would have been to anticipate their incapacity to deal with the subject before they had made the attempt. Job does not make answer to Elihu as he had done to the friends, because he is convinced of the truth of what he says, and he has therefore nothing to reply.

The LORD makes no allusion to Elihu, when he subsequently expresses his approval of Job and passes censure on his friends, because he was not one of the parties to the strife which was to be adjusted. He was not one of the contestants respecting whom a verdict was to be rendered, but an arbiter, whose decision the LORD assumes as preliminary to his own. It would not have comported with the divine dignity, for the infinite God to place himself on a level with his dependent creature, and enter into an argument with him in justification of his own sovereign acts, as though he were amenable to human judgement. As far, therefore, as there was any occasion for arguing the case with Job, and correcting his misapprehensions or vindicating the divine proceedings, this was committed to Elihu, who could meet Job as an equal and reason out the case with him, showing him that he was wrong, and that God was right.

This course was adopted likewise from a consideration of what was really best for Job himself. There was no divine terror to appal him, no effulgence of the infinite majesty to overwhelm him. Elihu came as the messenger of God to plead God's cause. Job could stand on a par with him and in a calm state of mind, and could make reply without irreverence, if the considerations presented did not convince his judgement. They were convincing. Job yielded to his arguments, and had no reply to make.

He tacitly confesses the justice of all that Elihu says. His false views are corrected; his misconceptions of God's providences toward him and of the design of God in his afflictions are removed. The way is thus prepared for the LORD to appear and, by the simple majesty of his divine perfections, to make the needed impression upon the heart of Job. The awe-struck patriarch bows at once in submissive penitence, for he has learned from Elihu to see in God no longer the impersonation of arbitrary power wielded for his destruction, but the God of grace, in whose hand even the rod of affliction was a means of blessing.

It appears that, though Elihu had not been spoken of before, he had been present during the discussion between Job and his three friends. He had said nothing, but had maintained throughout a respectful silence. This suggests the probability of the presence of others as well. The fame of the patriarch's sorrows had gone far and wide. And as after his restoration 'all his brothers, all his sisters, and all those who had been his acquaintances before, came to him and ate food with him in his house; and they consoled him and comforted him for all the adversity that the LORD had brought upon him' (42:11); so doubtless they did while his sorrows lasted.

Of this company of sympathizing friends, Eliphaz, Bildad and Zophar were the spokesmen, to whom the rest deferred as their superiors in age and in reputed wisdom. In the presence of this interested group the discussion had been conducted with the issue already recited. The friends had shown themselves unable to still Job's complaint or to answer his arguments. They could only vindicate the righteousness of God's providence by casting an aspersion on the character of his righteous servant.

So far it might appear as though Job's complaint were justified. Upon the principles of his friends, and upon any theory that he could frame for himself, God had done him wrong. He was treating him as though he were guilty of offences which he had not committed. The mystery that overhung the present case, and which involved the ways of providence in general, was still unsolved. Neither the friends nor Job could penetrate it or remove it. Must it remain forever insoluble?

Elihu had waited in the expectation that the three friends would bring out the true moral reasons of the distresses that befall good men like Job and would show the harmony of the perfections of God with his providential government. As, however, they failed to do this, he could no longer be restrained by his deference for these venerable sages, but was irresistibly impelled to speak. If the surmise be correct, that the kindred of Ram, to which he is said to have belonged, was the same as Aram, he came from a different region from the three friends, and there may be a significance that should not be overlooked in the mention of the fact.

Eliphaz and Teman were names perpetuated in the territory of Edom (*Gen.* 36:10,11), and the Shuhite recalls the children of Keturah, who were settled in the East country (*Gen.* 25:2, 6): all belonged to a region renowned for the wisdom and sagacity of its inhabitants. But Elihu comes, it may be, from a territory with associations of a different sort. When Balak was in straits, and felt the need of a higher than human help or counsel, he sent to Aram (*Num.* 23:7) for one who heard the words of God and knew the knowledge of the Most High and saw the vision of the Almighty (*Num.* 24:16). It was from Aram that Abraham came, the friend of God; and the epithet, the Buzite, reminds us of Buz in the family of Nahor, Abraham's brother (*Gen.* 22:21). It is not impossible that there may lie in these names[1] the suggestion of a land of divine intervention or immediate divine revelation, as opposed to the land of the highest earthly wisdom.

The representatives of the land of sages first confront the enigma, but are baffled: the resources of human reason are inadequate to the task. Then Elihu comes as the messenger of God. He is but a youth, with no pretensions to superior sagacity, and without the age that ordinarily brings wisdom and experience, but the inspiration of the Almighty had given him understanding (32:8). And he unravels the mystery which the venerable and the wise could not rightly expound. The wisdom of man is at an utter loss. That of God is alone competent to relieve the difficulty. 'God will vanquish him, not man' (32:13)

Elihu begins with an apology for speaking which may seem repetitious and prolix. But this arises from the diffidence of youth and inexperience in the presence of aged and venerable men, which made him feel as though he could not affirm too strongly nor repeat too often his reluctance to obtrude himself or his own views upon them. But an inward constraint that he could not resist, compelled him to declare

---

[1] If an appropriateness were to be sought in the personal names, Eliphaz might be explained to mean *God separates* or *divides*, and thus be linked with his fundamental tenet of a providential discrimination between the good and the bad. It is formed from a verb which is used of separating gold from dross. Elihu may mean *God is* or *God himself*; and he gives a truer doctrine of God and one which more accurately represents the divine Being. And he is the son of Barachel, *blessing God*, or *whom God blesses*.

the truth which had not thus far been uttered, and to return to Job the proper answer which had not yet been given. He promises that his treatment of the theme shall be perfectly impartial and unbiased: without respect of persons and without flattery, but with a single regard to the judgement of his Maker, he will hold an even balance between the friends and Job. He proposes to put the matter on an entirely new basis, one altogether different from that on which it had been placed by the friends, and against which Job had successfully aimed his arguments:

> Now he has not directed *his* words against me;
> So I will not answer him with your words (32:14).

That which chiefly distressed Job was that God seemed to be treating him as an enemy. He had dwelt most pathetically upon this aspect of his case, and had recited his dreadful sorrows as so many evidences of the fierceness of God's anger and the bitterness of his hostility. It was this which was so unaccountable to him and so dreadful. It is to the disabusing of his mind on this point, which was his radical error, that Elihu first and mainly addresses himself. Affliction, he tells him, is not a token of God's displeasure, but one of the measures of his grace. It is not sent in wrath, but with a kind and merciful design. It is one of the ways in which God speaks to men to draw them away from sin and to promote their highest welfare.

There are two principal methods, as he explains, which God employs in dealing with men, to detach them from what is wrong and establish them in what is pure and good; namely, his word and his providence. The former is described in terms appropriate to the period when Job lived which was prior to a written revelation, when one of the most usual forms in which immediate divine communications were made:

> In a dream, in a vision of the night,
> When deep sleep falls upon men,
> While slumbering on their beds,

Then He opens the ears of men,
And seals their instruction.
In order to turn man *from his* deed,
And conceal pride from man (33:15–17).

By these sacred instructions God saves from sin, and from the punishment which sin would involve:

He keeps back his soul from the Pit,
And his life from perishing by the sword (33:18).

Now, as he further goes on to say, God uses affliction for the same gracious end. He sends sickness and suffering to recall men to the path of uprightness. And then if the sufferer recognizes this merciful intent of his sorrows, and yields himself up to it, his pains will be removed. Their whole design will be accomplished, and they will be needed no more.

This is an entirely new doctrine, and exhibits the matter under a totally different aspect. The friends had seen in suffering nothing but the punishment of sin, and the divine displeasure against it. To Job's mind it was an arbitrary infliction, irrespective of men's deserts. But the idea of a gracious purpose in earthly distresses, the idea that they betoken the divine benignity and love, and are meant to accomplish a kindly end, had not dawned upon either of them.

Eliphaz indeed in his first and most gentle speech approaches so nearly to it, and uses expressions so akin to those of Elihu, that to a hasty and superficial view their doctrine might appear identical. He speaks (5:17) of the blessedness of the man whom God corrects, and bids Job not to despise the chastening of the Almighty:

For He bruises, but He binds up;
He wounds, but His hands make whole (5:18).

This looks to the possibility of good results following upon affliction, which may so far counterbalance the evil that he may be pronounced happy who endures it. And God who now sends sorrow, may hereafter send joy. Nevertheless suffering is to Eliphaz in its proper nature punitive, and represents God's displeasure against sin; while in the estimate of Elihu it is curative, and represents God's affectionate concern for the true welfare of the sufferer.

These two ideas are wide as the poles asunder. On the one view, God in afflicting a man regards him as a sinner, and treats him as such: his sufferings are tantamount to a sentence of condemnation. On the other, God regards rather his capacity for goodness, and seeks his purification and improvement. The development of the doctrine of the friends led directly to their gross and unfounded charges of hypocrisy and guilt. That of Elihu is perfectly consistent with Job's true character as affirmed by God himself; and it quite disarms Job by showing that he has been neither unkindly nor unjustly dealt with. God is not treating him as a criminal nor as a foe, as he supposed, but is showing a solicitous regard for his highest good.

The suggestion of Elihu as to the divine purpose in suffering is additional to that which is stated in the opening of the book as the occasion of the sorrows of Job; but it is not inconsistent with it, nor is it excluded by it. Though it was permitted at the instigation of Satan, who sought Job's hurt, it does not follow that the LORD had no designs of his own in granting the permission. Undoubtedly one design of God was to exhibit the reality of Job's piety, and its adequacy to bear the test, terrible as it was, which Satan proposed. But nothing obliges us to believe that God's merciful purpose was simply commensurate with the mischievous intention of the fiend, and that it was limited to thwarting and defeating the harm concocted for his servant.

Why may he not likewise have had positive designs of good which Satan's malice was, by overruling grace, to be made the instrument of effecting? Elihu declares that he had. And we have already seen good evolving to Job out of this seeming evil; and there is yet more to be brought out of it hereafter. Job is purified and instructed: his piety is heightened, and his knowledge of divine things is increased by this affliction. So that the doctrine of Elihu, far from conflicting with the rest of the book, finds in it ample justification and support. It was the purpose of God from the first to bless Job by means of this trial. And although this purpose has not been previously announced, until it is formally stated by Elihu, it is already gradually working itself out, and we shall see fuller fruits of it in that which follows.

That Job was put on trial was not stated to himself, for it was not the truth he needed to hear. But now that he has successfully borne the test, he needs to know the end of this infliction, not so far as Satan was concerned, but its end for himself. He needs to know that it was sent with a gracious design, and that it enclosed a real benefit. It was necessary that he should understand this, in order that he might be thoroughly released out of the tempter's snare, and might receive the full profit that was in store for him.

Elihu's doctrine of suffering is not hampered by the rigid and inflexible rule of exact retributive justice maintained by the friends; nor does it conflict, as that did, with the general facts of providence or with the consciousness of Job. Job's arguments and protests against the friends do not lie against it. It is a view, in fact, against which he has no disposition either to argue or to protest. It is not only consistent with, but gives a satisfactory account of the inequalities of the human condition.

The unbending rule of strict justice would have required a uniform and precise correspondence of men's fortunes with their characters. It admitted to no deviation. There might, indeed, be temporary delays. The divine retribution might be for a while postponed, but it must never fail to be ultimately and palpably meted out to all, in the true proportion of their merits and demerits.

But a gracious purpose is from its very nature free: It can be bound by no rule but the disposition and will of him who exercises it. The only limitation upon a providence so conducted is God's good pleasure; and none can prescribe in advance where he shall send joy or where he shall send sorrow. He may by his goodness lead men to repentance. He may employ chastisement to wean them from the love of this world or to turn their hearts from sin. The method employed in each particular instance depends solely upon his sovereign will. This admits all the free variety found in the actual experience of men, while at the same time it neither divorces the world from God nor represents his dealings as capricious and arbitrary. He without whom not a sparrow falls, numbers the hairs of our heads, directs all that concerns us, appoints all our lot. He governs in all the affairs of men, and he does so in a manner worthy of himself.

There is a method in all that occurs, and a purpose and a divine intelligence. Providence is harmonized with the infinite rectitude and the universal moral government. It becomes in fact the expression, the visible manifestation of God's holiness as well as of his grace; for it is directed with the view of reclaiming men from sin and training them in holiness and virtue. It is not graduated by any formal mechanical rule of correspondence with men's deserts, but it is wisely adapted, nevertheless, to their multiform needs by him whose resources are endless, and whose understanding is without a bound.

This doctrine likewise supplies the hitherto undiscovered key to the enigma of Job's sufferings. No reflection is cast upon his integrity or the genuineness of his piety. His afflictions are neither an indication of the LORD's displeasure nor of his wanton hostility. A gracious God is by this severity of discipline purging away the dross which still adhered to his faithful servant, and refining the gold to a higher measure of purity.

Accordingly, when Elihu pauses in his discourse (33:32) to afford Job an opportunity for reply, he makes none. He has nothing to say in opposition to what he has heard. He has no answer to make. It has wrought conviction in his soul. It has composed the strife which previously agitated him. It has reconciled the conflicting opposites. It harmonizes his convictions respecting God with what has hitherto been inexplicable in his providence. It makes all plain in his own case, which has thus far been so dark and impenetrable. God has not been impeaching his integrity by these terrible sufferings which he has inflicted or permitted. God has not been charging upon him a guilt of which the testimony of his own conscience acquits him. Nor has he been treating him with causeless and gratuitous severity. There is no hostile intent on the part of God: All has been done in kindness and in love.

The truth evidences itself to him by its adaptation to all the exigencies of the case in hand. It finds a prompt echo in Job's own heart and he bows in mute acquiescence to the force of what has been said. He is no longer roused to opposition as by the language of his friends, whom he has reduced to silence. He is now himself silenced in his turn. He owns and feels the justice and propriety of the view which has been propounded, and he listens in silent acknowledgement of its truth. Elihu has not only gained his ear, but his heart; and the solution of the mystery, which has so baffled and perplexed him, begins to open before him.

Having established his main position, Elihu proceeds (34:35) to comment upon some of Job's ill-considered and hasty utterances, which fell from him in the heat of his controversy with his friends. They were incessantly representing the justice of God as hopelessly at war with the idea of the integrity of Job. Not seeing, in the desperate gloom that enveloped him, how this conclusion was to be escaped, Job boldly admits it, and in the thorough consciousness of his own rectitude is driven to affirm that God has done him wrong.

But now that this antagonism has been done away by the new principle which Elihu has announced, Job is no longer under any temptation to dispute the righteousness of God's providential administration. Elihu accordingly holds up before him some of his most extravagant assertions, and points out their absurdity and impropriety. In saying (34:5; cf. 37:2), 'God has taken away my justice', despoiled me of my rights, treated me unjustly, Job was consorting with wicked men, and loosening the foundations of God's universal government. Shall not the judge of all the earth do right? It is repugnant to every notion of propriety to charge the supreme and all-perfect Ruler with injustice.

If a conflict arise between God and his creatures, whom he can be under no possible temptation to injure, the overwhelming presumption, nay, the absolute certainty, is that he is right and they are wrong, whether they can see it to be so or not:

> For has *anyone* said to God,
> 'I have borne *chastening*;
> I will offend no more;
> Teach me *what* I do not see;
> If I have done iniquity, I will do no more' (34:31–32).

'Do you think this is right?' he adds (35:2),

> Do you say [not in so many words, indeed, but in substance],
> 'My righteousness is more than God's'?

when you are but a trifling, insignificant creature, of no account compared with the infinite Creator?

Job had invariably resented such language before from his friends. Their appeals to God's righteousness always exasperated him, for the necessary implication from it, as presented by them, was that he was a guilty man, who deserved all that he suffered. Sensitive as he might properly be to unjust imputations, he was indignant at these indirect reproaches.

But in the mouth of Elihu it is different. It contains no covert censure of himself. The assertion of God's inviolable justice veils no aspersions or insinuations. The simple truth of the perfection of the ever-blessed God stands alone before him in its innate majesty, and free from all distortions or false conclusions, and its reality cannot but be confessed. Job cannot oppose what is so self-evident. He continues to bow in silent acquiescence.

Elihu, having thus corrected Job's errors and reproved the rash speeches into which he had in consequence been betrayed, reverts again to his fundamental principle of the design of suffering, making special application of it to the case of Job, and basing upon it a faithful admonition (36:1–33). Afflictions, he repeats, are sent upon the righteous for their good; and such an experience is fraught with solemn responsibility to the afflicted themselves. If they recognize the gracious purpose of God in their sorrows, and heed the lesson they involve, then the design of this painful dispensation will be accomplished, and it will be itself removed.

If, on the contrary, they disregard the voice of love and warning which speaks to them in these distresses, they will incur the divine displeasure, and bring God's judgement on themselves in the form of still heavier sorrows than they have yet experienced. Thus, he tells Job, it will be with him. He might have found deliverance already, if he had profited sufficiently by the teachings of his sad calamities and learned from them to be more diligent in avoiding sin, and to cleave more unreservedly to the service of the LORD.

Elihu has now fulfilled the task assigned to him. He was charged with removing misapprehensions from Job's mind and correcting the mistakes into which he had fallen. But it was not given to him to extricate Job entirely, out of Satan's snare, and accomplish for him the full and blessed effects of his temptation. This work the LORD reserved for himself, to be performed by him in his own person. Elihu is but his messenger sent before his face to prepare his way before him. And now even while he is speaking the rumbling is heard of distant thunder (37:2); heavy masses of cloud begin to darken the sky, and the advancing tempest betokens the LORD's approach. Elihu points to these insignia of the divine Majesty as they steadily draw near, and his own voice is hushed in awe. All are mute in solemn expectation. It is the LORD who comes.

IO

The LORD

Then the LORD *answered Job out of the whirlwind, and said: 'Who is this who darkens counsel by words without knowledge?'* (Job 38:1–2).

We have now come to what is beyond all comparison the most sublime portion of this wonderful book. All the discourses hitherto, whether of Job or of the other speakers, have been well conceived and admirably expressed. They present their profound and earnest thoughts with singular beauty and force. They glow with elegant and appropriate imagery. And they present in vividly graphic language the inward excitement and changing emotions of those by whom they are uttered. All had been well and ably spoken. But now when the LORD himself speaks to Job, his discourse is fitly marked by a grandeur and a majesty altogether unequalled before, and which is worthy of the divine Being.

It might upon the first superficial view of the case appear as though the discourse of the LORD had no particular relevance to the circumstances in which it was uttered. And the question might arise what these appeals to the magnificence of the works of God in nature have to do with the solution of the enigma to which this book is devoted. How do they contribute to the explanation of the mystery that is involved in the sufferings of good men?

The fact is, this discourse is not directed to an elucidation of that mystery at all. It is not the design of God to offer a vindication of his dealings with men in general, or a justification of his providence towards Job. He has no intention of placing himself at the bar of his creatures and elevating them into judges of his conduct. He is not amenable to them and he does not recognize their right to be censors of him and of his ways.

REALITY CHECK

The righteousness of his providence does not depend upon their perceiving or admitting it. The LORD does not here stand on the defensive, not allowing it to seem as if he were in any need of being relieved from the strictures of Job, or as if it were of any account to him whether feeble worms approved his dealings or confessed the propriety of his dispensations. He puts himself in a totally different attitude, and moves upon quite another plane. He is the sovereign LORD of all, accountable to no being but himself. He does not appear to vindicate himself, but to rescue Job.

Job has been exposed to the fierce assaults of Satan and has successfully withstood them. The tempter employed all his power and all his craft to bring him to forsake the service of the LORD; but he remained firm in his steadfastness nevertheless. The reality and the strength of Job's piety were conspicuously established from the moment that he uttered his memorable declaration, 'I know that my Redeemer lives' (19:25). His heroic trust in God was not destroyed by the direst calamities, nor even by the wrathful frowns that seemed to darken his face. Job was fully vindicated against Satan's baseless slander.

But the affair was not to be terminated there. It was not the divine purpose that the trial should end with this merely negative result. Nor was it enough that he should simply receive the profit, which had already arisen to him from the struggle through which he had been obliged to pass. His constancy and faith have been heightened. He has grown in spiritual heroism and power. He has risen to clearer and broader views than he possessed before. And practice has taught him skill: He has learned how to overcome temptation by actual experience.

But even this was not all. The LORD had still larger designs of good in store for his faithful servant. The true vindication of God's providence lies in the event. It must not be judged by the confused and tangled threads which it seems to present to the beholder while in the process of being wrought, but by the completed pattern when all shall be finished. The LORD has been in no haste to justify himself by a premature disclosure of his plans. He has suffered things to move regularly forward and to take their appointed course. But now the time has arrived for his own intervention to bring the matter to its intended termination.

Satan had been allowed to bring a double evil upon Job, in his outward circumstances and in his spiritual state. He had inflicted severe external losses and sufferings and he had involved him in a sore inward conflict. Job had fought through the latter victoriously, so far as it was possible for him to do from his previous standpoint in religious knowledge and in the religious life. He had risen to the sublime assurance that God was his Redeemer and friend, and would be, let come what would. No floods of temptation could destroy this conviction, no fierceness of Satan's assault could wrest it from him.

But still the cloud and the mystery remained. A disturbing element had been introduced into the patriarch's inward experience, which he could defy so as to hold fast to his faith in God in spite of it, but which was nevertheless productive of disquiet and distress. He could not attain to that placid, unruffled state of calm repose which marked his condition before his trials came. There had been a jar in his relations to his Maker, which, though it could not throw him off his firm foundation, had yet marred his tranquillity and peace. But this disturbance was not to last always.

It had been a valuable discipline to Job in two respects. He had in the first place, as we have seen, been instructed and strengthened by the intensity of the struggle which had been forced upon him. And in addition, he had been prepared to receive a further spiritual lesson. He had been made aware of a need which he did not previously know to exist – a need of instruction, a need of succour, which craved a heavenly gift that had before been unsought because the necessity which required it had not been felt. He was now in a state of readiness to welcome a new divine communication; and this had been brought about by the trials through which he had passed.

Satan meant to have sundered him from the LORD. In fact, he opened the way for larger and fuller impartations of divine knowledge and grace. He had but prepared the way of the LORD, who was now to come to Job with a nearness and fulness of manifestation as never before.

The sore discipline of Job had endured long enough. It had wrought its full effect of preparation for the divine intervention. The LORD, therefore, appears upon the scene without further delay, to perfect the blessing which, as he has all along intended, was to be the issue of his severe but salutary trials. He comes to rescue him from the double distress in which Satan has plunged him, and to bestow upon him a corresponding twofold benefit – first, inward and spiritual; second, outward and temporal.

The LORD first produces an effect upon the heart of Job. He makes such a manifestation of himself to the sufferer's soul as brings him to the deepest humiliation and contrition for all his rash and impatient utterances and all the improper reflections he had cast upon God's dealings with him in his providence. He had before found peace with his Maker, so far as his personal relation to God was concerned. But now he is entirely acquiescent in all the LORD's dealings. He repents of his murmurings. He surrenders his wayward resistance to the divine orderings. His will is henceforth coincident with the divine will and completely swallowed up in it. And he is amazed at himself and filled with self-abhorrence that it ever could have been otherwise with him.

Thereupon the LORD, in addition, restores Job's outward estate and raises it to a higher measure of prosperity than he possessed before. The whole matter is thus brought to its final issue, Job's piety is elevated and his welfare and happiness are promoted. The latter is recorded in the historical paragraph which concludes the book, the last eleven verses of the final chapter. The former is accomplished by the LORD's discourse, which does not do its work, however, by means of arguments addressed to the solution of the enigma that has occupied the minds of Job and of his friends. This discourse contains a solution only in so far as it is effective in bringing about that result, which is itself the explanation of this mysterious providence.

The purpose of the LORD's discourse in its relation to Job and to the problem of the afflictions of the righteous has been variously misconceived and mis-stated. As it is chiefly occupied with appeals to the works of God in nature, which display in such a striking manner the omnipotence of the Most High in its contrast with the impotence of man, it has been thought that the main idea, reiterated in various forms and enforced throughout this address, is the infinite exaltation and power of God. His sway is irresistible. It is vain to think of opposing omnipotence. And the lesson thence deduced is supposed to be that of unconditional resignation to the will of the Infinite Sovereign.

Since God is almighty, his orderings must be submitted to. The creature must yield unresistingly to what the Creator decrees. It is worse than useless to repine or murmur: man must bow with meek submission to anything allotted from such a source, be it what it may.

But submission to the inevitable is stoicism, or fatalism, not scriptural resignation. We have to do not with overwhelming force, but with our heavenly Father, who demands our love as well as our willing obedience; and to whom we should submit not by constraint, but with a ready mind. We may be compelled to yield subjection to irresistible power, but it will not satisfy the reason nor the sense of right.

It was this, in fact, which lent its chief aggravation to the temptation of Job; this was the very point about which it all centred. His unaccountable sufferings, the baseless reasonings of his friends, and everything in his whole situation, conspired to set the LORD before him in the aspect of a Being of absolute and arbitrary power who was using his omnipotence to torture and destroy him without any ground in reason or any relentings of pity. An almighty tyrant on the throne of the universe would inspire terror but could not awaken confidence or love.

He might break down all open opposition and stamp out the very semblance of it, but he could not compel the adoration of the heart. Job, prostrate and bleeding, protested with what he supposed to be his dying breath against the cruel wrong which was done him. Violence, from which there is no escape and against which there is no remedy, is only the more dreaded and detested on that account. God is more than almighty power or Job would not have humbled himself before him as he did in cordial homage and submissive self-abasement. He fell prostrate before an inward constraint which was very different from outward compulsion.

Again it has been supposed that the burden of the LORD's discourse is God's infinite wisdom as displayed in his works, which so far transcends our faculties, baffling the most adventurous efforts of the human understanding. These appeals to the incomprehensible marvels which everywhere abound in the world are intended, it is said, to suggest the existence of marvels equally incomprehensible in God's providence. There is a mystery in all his ways, in nature, and

in the affairs of men, which no human intelligence is able
to penetrate. It must be accepted as a product of the infinite
reason without insisting upon knowing how or why. It is
not given to man to fathom what belongs only to the divine
understanding to comprehend. The ways of God are
inscrutable. Man should adore where he cannot understand,
and submit without questioning to anything apportioned,
which it would be arrogant to suppose could be made level
to his feeble comprehension.

There is a partial truth in this view as in the preceding
point. God is infinitely wise and infinitely powerful and both
of these attributes of the divine nature supply considerations
which enter into and enforce pious resignation. But the
lesson of the book of Job in these most solemn utterances
from the mouth of God himself is something more than that
there is nothing we can know and that the mystery of the
sufferings of good men must remain unexplained, for no
explanation is possible.

This would not set at rest troubled questionings and
anxious inquiries into the principles of the divine administration, and its consistency with God's ineffable perfections.
It would rather tend to repel all inquiry as profitless and
leading to no certain or safe result, even if it is not positively
profane - a pernicious treading on forbidden ground, and a
prying into what it is not allowable to know. Instead, then, of
shedding any light upon this mysterious subject, the only
teaching of this book would be that we must remain content
with a darkness that can never, from the nature of the case, be
dispelled. Instead of adding to our knowledge it would
declare that further knowledge was unattainable.

And, if this were the case, why should the LORD have
revealed himself to Job at all in so august a manner? In what
respect was he helped or instructed by the manifestation of
God to him, if it had no other intent than that just stated? If
the discourse of the LORD, with all its rare sublimity, does not
carry him beyond the point which he had already reached
himself, what was the need of any immediate divine

intervention? Job was profoundly sensible of the mystery of God's providence. And he had confessed it to be quite impenetrable. The wisdom that could fathom it, he had said, was 'hidden from the eyes of all living' (28:21) and was possessed by God alone. So the highest wisdom to which man could attain was the fear of the LORD (33:20–28). Job had learned to adhere to his pious fear of God, though he could not comprehend his ways; to acknowledge the LORD to be his Redeemer, though his providence remained an incomprehensible mystery. The lesson of the LORD's discourse must be something beyond what Job had himself already attained to.

There are two things which may supply the key to what this lesson really is: The first is the preliminary speech of Elihu, by which that of the LORD is immediately preceded; and the second, the effect which the latter produces upon Job.

The LORD's discourse is not to be sundered from that of Elihu, which was the preparation for it, which was followed by it without any pause and thus, as it were, merged into it, and which was taken for granted by it. Elihu was sent with the theoretical answer to the great problem to which the LORD supplied the practical solution. Elihu was commissioned to make the needed explanations to Job, to rectify his mistakes and point out to him wherein he had erred. His task was to disabuse his mind of every false impression and prepare him for the coming of the LORD, so that upon his appearance he might instantly recognize him in his true character, and feel toward him as he should.

To Job's mind his sufferings had been hostile treatment on the part of God. He could look upon them in no other light than as tokens of the divine displeasure. God was dealing with him in anger. He was indeed able notwithstanding to affirm that God was his Redeemer. In spite of his present hostility, which was so unaccountable and so distressing, Job had gained the confident assurance that God would yet at some future time lay aside these strangely mysterious frowns and manifest himself on his behalf. But Elihu opens up to him a new view of the case. He shows him that this imagined hostility is not really such. His afflictions are not the fruit of God's anger, but of his kindness and love. God has not been dealing hardly and cruelly with him, but has been accomplishing the purposes of his grace on his behalf by methods which, however severe, are salutary.

This alters the whole aspect of the matter. What had been dark before is dark no longer. The face of God seems no more to wear a forbidding aspect even for a season. What he had thought to be the terrible seizure of a mortal foe is the powerful grasp of a friend. What he had imagined to be the deadly thrust of hostile weapons proves to be the skilful incision of the great physician who wounds but to heal. His repinings and murmurings and bitter complaints have no longer any foundation.

The chief source of his agitation and distress is gone. The seeming contradiction has vanished between the actual and the ideal, between what he experienced and he might have expected, between the God of the present and of the future, between the God who afflicts and the God who saves. God is his Redeemer, not merely out of existing sorrows or in spite of them, but in them and through them and by means of them. Faith is no longer reduced to such straits that it can barely maintain itself by looking away from the present and holding fast to the unseen future. It has a visible and tangible basis in the present itself. In these very trials which had threatened to sweep away his trust in God, that trust now finds a new and firm support; for he discerns in them the clear tokens of heavenly love.

The cloud has disappeared which for a time had hidden the bright shining of his Father's face. And now when God manifests himself to Job, there is nothing to obscure his sense of the divine favour and loving-kindness. The distorted image of God has passed away completely and forever. Ineffable love is restored to its true place among the perfections of the Most High. His might and greatness do not stand alone. He who is infinite in these is infinite likewise in his compassions. It is sufficient to point out any indication of the LORD's presence or of the grandeur of his being, to bring all the divine attributes full-orbed before the mind of Job. He sees the LORD no longer through a false medium, which shuts out half the glory of his nature, but as he truly is.

The same thing appears from the effect which the LORD's discourse produces upon Job. It gives him a new and more distinct apprehension of God, a more vivid and powerful impression of his glorious nature. It was not the perception of one attribute isolated from the rest, or exalted above the rest, which led him to exclaim:

> I have heard of You by the hearing of the ear,
> But now my eye sees You (42:5).

All his previous conceptions of God were faint and distant compared with the intimate and thorough conviction of his exalted being which now possessed his soul. It was like something which is learned by distant report compared with what stands revealed with the clearness and evidence of eyesight. This points to no partial, imperfect, one-sided view of God, in which certain attributes are made prominent at the expense of others, and some are hidden altogether, but to a complete and true perception of God in his real character. His impatient utterances under the pressure of his afflictions were due to a defective apprehension of the glorious character of God. Now that he sees God as he truly is, he is abashed and confounded that he ever could have spoken as he did or indulged such feelings as he then had.

The LORD's discourse was spoken with the aim of producing this effect upon Job and bringing him to this humbled and repentant state of mind. The important fact, and that which is really influential in the case, is that God now manifests himself to the soul of Job; and this discourse is simply an accompaniment or a medium of this manifestation. It opens up to Job and brings home to him in the most impressive manner the greatness and the perfection of that being with whom he has to do. The whole address is but the unfolding of the thought, 'I am the infinite, and all-perfect God.' And this truth is set before his mind by a series of appeals to the grandeur of God's works, by which his perfections are so strikingly displayed in contrast with the utter insignificance of man. Job is made to feel at once who it is that is speaking to him; and how completely he had stepped out of his province, and of what incredible arrogance and presumption he had been guilty in venturing to pass his judgement upon the doings of the Most High.

'Then the LORD answered Job out of the whirlwind' (38:1). The clouds, to which Elihu had pointed as covering the light had grown darker and more threatening until they overspread the sky. The lightening, the thunder, and the tempest, in which the LORD had veiled his awful majesty, had been steadily approaching, and filled all hearts with solemn dread. And now from the bosom of the rushing storm comes forth a voice, the voice of Jehovah, in unapproachable sublimity, speaking unto Job:

> Who is this who darkens counsel
> By words without knowledge? (38:2).

Who and what is he who has been daring to obscure the wise orderings of my gracious and holy providence by the ignorant and empty reflections he has cast upon them? What is his ability, and what his claims to act as the censor of the divine proceedings?

> Now prepare yourself like a man;
> I will question you, and you shall answer Me.
> Where were you when I laid the foundations of the earth?
> Tell *Me*, if you have understanding.
> Who determined its measurements?
> Surely you know!
> Or who stretched the line upon it?
> To what were its foundations fastened?
> Or who laid its cornerstone,
> When the morning stars sang together,
> And all the sons of God shouted for joy?

Or *who* shut in the sea with doors,
When it burst forth *and* issued from the womb;
When I made the clouds its garment,
And thick darkness its swaddling band;
When I fixed my limit for it,
And set bars and doors;
When I said,
'This far you may come, but no farther,
And here your proud waves must stop!'
Have you commanded the morning since your days *began*,
And caused the dawn to know its place? (38:4–12).

The LORD further continues his appeal to the marvels of
the sea, of death and the unseen world, of light and darkness,
of the snow and rain, the ice and cold, of the stars, of the
various celestial changes with their terrestrial effects, of the
soul of man, of the instincts, habits, and adaptations of
various orders of the animate creation; and concludes with
the pointed interrogation:

Shall the one who contends with the Almighty correct *Him*?
He who rebukes God, let him answer it (40:2).

Awe-struck and abashed at his own littleness and at the
absurd pretensions involved in his rash and inconsiderate
complaints, Job answered the LORD and said:

Behold, I am vile;
What shall I answer You?
I lay my hand over my mouth.
Once I have spoken, but I will not answer;
Yes, twice, but I will proceed no further (40:4–5).

The LORD then speaks once more to Job with the view of
deepening the impression already made, and of showing still
further of what vain conceit of his own powers Job had been
guilty, and what unheard-of assumptions were involved in the
language he had suffered himself to use. Was he prepared to
assume the government of the world, and to take it out of the
hands of the Most High, whose administration he had
ventured to arraign? God challenges him to show a power or

execute deeds of judgement which would warrant these bold
pretensions.

> Would you indeed annul my judgment?
> Would you condemn Me that you may be justified?
> Have you an arm like God?
> Or can you thunder with a voice like His?
> Then adorn yourself *with* majesty and splendor,
> And array yourself with glory and beauty.
> Disperse the rage of your wrath;
> Look on everyone *who is* proud, and humble him.
> Look on everyone *who is* proud, *and* bring him low;
> Tread down the wicked in their place.
> Hide them in the dust together,
> Bind their faces in hidden *darkness*.
> Then I will also confess to you
> That your own right hand can save you (40:8–14).

So far indeed is he from being able to measure himself with
God that he cannot even cope with his creatures, as he
is reminded by a reference to two formidable animals,
behemoth and leviathan, perhaps the hippopotamus and
crocodile.

The full impression intended has by this time been made
on Job, and he falls prostrate before the infinite God in self-
abasement and self-reproach. Convicted of his fault, he makes
instant confession:

> Therefore I have uttered what I did not understand,
> Things too wonderful for me, which I did not know . . .
> I have heard of You by the hearing of the ear,
> But now my eye sees You.
> Therefore I abhor *myself*,
> And repent in dust and ashes (42:3, 5–6).

Job has now reached an elevation far above his former self.
The depth of his humiliation is really the summit of his
exaltation in piety and in the fear and love of God. That he
now looks down upon himself as he does, shows how he has
been raised above what he was before. He has made a great

advance beyond the fervour of that moment when, in the darkest period of his struggle, his faith looked out with more than eagle-glance into the unseen, and by one mighty effort rose superior to every temptation based upon the visible and the temporal, affirming God to be his Redeemer in the face of everything outward which seemed to forbid all hope. The faith, to which he has now attained, would not only have gained the mastery in this frightful contest, but would have trampled Satan's temptation under foot without a conflict.

The faith, which shone out so conspicuously in that triumphant exclamation, was nevertheless defective, or the struggle would not have been so fierce, nor the triumph so hard to gain. He trusted in God, who was afflicting him, so far as steadfastly to believe and to declare that God would certainly hereafter, in the world to come, if not in this, lay aside his seeming hostility and reveal himself as his friend. He trusted in God in spite of these afflictions, confident that he would deliver him out of them and would then be his God.

But his trust in God was not such as to persuade him that in afflicting him he was still acting as his gracious God and Redeemer. He was so far under the dominion of sense that there was still a region which faith had not completely subdued unto itself. The opposition between God's present treatment of him and his loving regard for him still remained to his mind, and he had not that implicit trust in God which could do it away.

He had a faith which could resolutely turn its back upon the mountain of difficulty, but not one which could say to it, 'Be removed, and be cast into the depths of the sea, and sunk out of sight or dissolved away beneath the ocean of divine love.' There still was to him an apparent contradiction here, which his faith could disregard, but could not annul; a present breach between him and God, which his faith could bridge over, but could not close up.

Now, however, he has learned to exercise a more perfect trust in God. He now confides in him more thoroughly than before. He can now trust God in everything, and believe that he does all things well. He has gained such a view of God and of the perfections of his being that he now believes that the Most High cannot do anything that is out of harmony with his perfections. All that he does must be right and wise and good.

Job's faith may not enable him to fathom the mysteries of God, nor to solve the riddles of his providence. He may not comprehend how these things are. But he knows that God is all-perfect and all-glorious, and he has that confidence in him which assures him that these things must be so. If he has sent affliction, this is not even a temporary interruption of his favour and love, though these are sure to shine forth again hereafter, clearly and fully. Nor is it enough to say that affliction is capable of being reconciled with the divine love. It is itself a fruit of that love. God is equally loving and gracious when he sends affliction and when he sends prosperous abundance.

Job's afflictions have not abated yet. His terrible losses are still as great as they were and his bodily sufferings are as grievous. But the cloud is gone. He has lost all disposition to murmur or repine. He is amazed at himself that he could ever have done so.

Since the LORD has disclosed himself to him, such a sense of his perfections, who is blessed for ever, has filled his soul that it forms the basis of an absolutely unlimited confidence. He can trust the infinitely holy and mighty and gracious one to do what seems good to him. It is good if God does it; it is the best thing possible.

No man at least, nor any finite being, could alter it for the better; and Job would not have it otherwise. The temptation is not vanquished now: it has disappeared. It is not overcome by a tremendous effort; but the huge mountain has sunk to a level plain. Though the sea roared before and was troubled, he went through the midst of its waves unharmed and dry-shod; but now his faith has gained in strength until it has been able to bid the sea become dry land; and the billows have ceased their tempestuous roll, and there is no more sea.

Job has come to the end of the third, which is the last and most fearful stage of the temptation. The struggle has been tremendous. It has been a long and a wearisome and a desperately contested conflict. But the issue is glorious. The forces of the enemy are not merely driven back, and left to rally and return again to the charge. They are not merely routed and put to an ignominious and disordered flight. They are positively annihilated, and the victory is complete and final.

Sublime as was Job's resignation in the first and second stage of his afflictions, it is sublimer now. When his property and his children were all swept from him at a stroke, Job still blessed the name of the LORD, mindful of the fact that the LORD had given what he now took away. When in addition his own person was visited with a dreadful and incurable malady, he meekly received the evil at the hands of the LORD, mindful of the good which he had previously bestowed.

His constant trust in God rooted itself each time in the past, in the abundance of former mercies, his grateful sense of which was not effaced by all the severity of his present trials. He put his trials in the scales over against the benefits which the LORD had so bounteously conferred upon him, and the latter still largely outweighed.

TRUE & VERY HUMAN.

Nevertheless each infliction of evil was an opposing weight, acting with whatever force it possessed in a contrary direction from God's mercies, and to that extent detracting from his sense of the divine goodness and love. This laid him open to the temptation of Satan. And it created the possibility that if weight enough could be accumulated on the side of affliction, acting as it did with the advantage which the immediate present, ever thrusting itself on the consciousness, has over the dim and fading sense of the more and more distant past, it might at length create an equipoise, and finally turn the scales the other way. And if this takes place, Job has fallen, and Satan has gained the victory.

During the most terrible period of his sorrows, when Satan seemed to have summoned every influence possible to depress the scales, Job was indeed hard pressed by his wily and unscrupulous foe, and was put to the greatest straits. It was as much as he could do, by straining his strength to the utmost, to maintain the balance on the right side. It was only by the strenuous efforts of a faith that took hold of the unseen, brought to its aid the world of the future, and laid its grasp upon the immutable attributes of God himself, thus pinning the scale down to the everlasting rock, that he could keep the balance on the side of God and piety against a pressure to great for nature to sustain.

And thus there was, to this extent, some foundation for Satan's malignant sneer, 'Does Job fear God for nothing?' (1:9) The enemy had detected a crevice in the structure of Job's faith, into which he hoped to drive a wedge that should rend the edifice asunder and bring it crumbling into ruins. Job's sense of God's goodness rested on the benefits received from him, instead of the divine goodness being itself the fixed foundation, and everything received from the hand of God being for that reason counted a benefit.

SENSIBLE UNDERSTANDING

He judged of God by his own partial and defective notion of his dealings, instead of judging those dealings by his knowledge of God. Job had, in the fierce conflict which Satan has waged against him, been driven by sheer necessity to base his faith on the immovable foundation, notwithstanding the darkness and confusion of mind which still rested upon the mysterious subject of his sufferings.

But now that Elihu had, as God's messenger of instruction, pointed out to him the gracious ends of affliction, and the LORD had revealed himself to him in the true glory of his nature, the previously existing flaw in Job's faith is closed up. The perfections of God have now become his first postulate, self-evidenced, and independent of any support to be derived from his particular dealings with him.

ATHEISTS SHOULD HEED

Heaven and earth may pass away. All things seen and temporal may fluctuate and change. But the perfections of God abide, incapable of mutation or decay. This is the one invariable fixed point, the basis of all certainty, and of all correct judgements. It is, in mathematical phrase, the origin to which everything is to be referred, and from which everything is to be estimated. God must ever act like himself. Whatever he does must be consistent with his glorious attributes, must be in fact the outflow of those attributes. The orderings of providence have their spring in the perfections of the ever-blessed God. Sense cannot discern this. But faith affirms it, and persistently adheres to it, be the outward appearance of things what it may.

WELL SAID

This is the lesson which Job has now learned; and hence he retracts all his murmuring words, and all that he has said reproachful to his Maker. He abhors himself for having uttered them, and repents in dust and ashes. He would not now ask as before, 'Shall we indeed accept good from God, and shall we not accept adversity?' (2:10). There is no adversity, there can be no adversity from the hand of the LORD.

HARD TO TELL ADVERSITY FROM JUDGEMENT. DIFFICULT.

Adversity is good when it comes from him. He no longer puts the benefits received from God in one scale and afflictions in the other. But afflictions are put in the same scale with benefits: they, too, are benefits when God sends them. And thus, instead of tending to create a counter-poise, they but add their weight to that of previously existing obligation.

The nerve of Satan's temptation is now cut completely. Every weight goes henceforth into the scale of God's goodness, and there is no possibility of disturbing the existing preponderance. He who has learned to place his sole and undivided trust in God, and to estimate all things by the standard of his perfection, is beyond the reach of any serious attempt to detach him from the LORD's service. To such a faith Job has risen under the felt power of God's immediate presence. He is now in a perfectly impregnable position, and Satan can assail him no longer. His spiritual deliverance is complete.

The LORD's purpose in permitting these dreadful sorrows is at length fully accomplished. There is no further occasion, therefore, for their continuance. Accordingly the LORD now interferes for their removal. And first he pronounces in Job's favour and against his friends. 'The LORD said to Eliphaz the Temanite, "My wrath is aroused against you and your two friends, for you have not spoken of Me what is right, as My servant Job has".' They had really indicted the providence of God by their professed defence of it. By disingenuously covering up and ignoring its enigmas and seeming contradictions, they had cast more discredit upon it than Job had by honestly holding them up to the light.

Their denial of its apparent inequalities was more untrue and more dishonouring to the divine administration, as it is in fact conducted, than Job's bold affirmation of them. Even his most startling utterances wrung from him in his bewilderment and sore perplexity were less reprehensible than their false statements and false inferences.

In averring that God was treating Job as a gross offender, they indirectly charge him with injustice and cruelty to his faithful servant. Job's impatient outcries under his sore distress were less offensive to God than these unwarrantable misrepresentations. And now that humbled and penitent he had retracted all that he had rashly spoken, everything was forgiven and forgotten but his present noble confession, in which, stricken as he was in the dust, and bleeding at every pore, he had yet placed God upon the throne, and submitted without a murmur to his holy will.

The friends of Job, who had thought him an outcast from the divine favour, can only be restored to that favour themselves through the intercession of their maligned and injured friend. This intercession is not withheld, for he bears no malice towards them, and no resentment for all their ill-treatment. The bitterness that had sometimes broken out in his former speeches is entirely gone. He forgives them as God had forgiven him. And with this renewed evidence of the profit which he had derived from his afflictions, his captivity is turned and his former prosperity is renewed and doubled.

Job is now entirely extricated from Satan's snare and released from his burden of woe. And the riddle is at length solved. The explanation of the sufferings of God's dear children, as suggested by the case of Job, may be embraced in the following particulars. They afford to all gainsayers a palpable test of their integrity. The very intensity of the struggle develops their faith and other graces, and leads them on to clearer views of heavenly truth. These sorrows are sent on the part of God with a gracious design, and afford the occasion of his revealing himself to chastened souls with new fitness and power, in consequence of which they are brought nearer to him than ever before, and their happiness and welfare are proportionally promoted.

The apostle James says: 'Indeed we count them blessed who endure. You have heard of the perseverance of Job and seen the end *intended by* the Lord – that the Lord is very compassionate and merciful' (*James* 5:11).

Appendices

1: The Place of the Book of Job
in the Scheme of Holy Scripture

Blessed are those who mourn, for they shall be comforted (Matt. 5:4).

We have now made our way, as we have been able, through the book of Job. We have traced the sore temptation which it describes, from its beginning through its successive stages until its ultimate removal. We have seen the part taken by each of the actors in this spiritual strife, Satan, Job's wife, his friends, Elihu, and the Lord.

We have observed Job's own demeanour through it all. And we have endeavoured to read the lessons of this mysterious dispensation as they are here suggested. Our task is not quite finished yet, however. If we would estimate this book aright, we must learn not only what it is, but to what it leads. Germs of truth are exhibited that were destined to be expanded subsequently. Lines of thought are started which, consistently followed out, conduct to far-reaching consequences. The sorrows of the man of Uz stand like the smitten rock of the desert at the head-waters of the stream of consolation. This precious tide flows on with ever-deepening current, gathering fresh tributaries as it flows, and bearing more abundant blessings on its bosom, until it issues in the boundless, unfathomable ocean of divine grace and love, within view of which we are brought in the gospel.

No book of the Bible stands apart by itself, or can be fully understood if it is only studied separately and in its isolation. It is part of a gradually unfolded revelation. It belongs to a well-ordered system. It is a link in a chain. It is a member of an organism. It is what it is, not for itself alone; it has been shaped with reference to the position that it is to occupy and the function it has to perform in the plan of the whole. The history of Job is one among a great body of signal facts, illustrative of God's ways with men and of his plan of grace.

The book of Job is one of a long series of inspired writings through which it has pleased God to make known his will and to reveal himself. What precise part does it take in the successive disclosures of divine truth? How does it advance upon what had before been made known? How does it prepare for what was to follow? What educating power lay in the truths which it lodged in the minds and hearts of men, and what further consequences did they produce? And how do its teachings stand related to the completed revelation of the gospel?

It would be impossible to treat exhaustively such a theme as this within the narrow limits to which we must confine ourselves and to attempt to do so under any circumstances might savour of arrogance and presumption. It will be sufficient to venture a few observations by way of suggestion.

The law precedes the gospel in logical order as in actual fact. It is thus in the experience of the race of man as a whole, in that of the chosen people, and in that of individual men. The covenant of works goes before the covenant of grace; the sentence upon our transgressing first parents before the promise of him who should bruise the serpent's head; the commandment given by Moses before grace and truth by

Jesus Christ; the conviction of sin before the apprehension of saving mercy. Unless the lesson of the just desert of sin and of the inflexible righteousness of God has first been learned, the necessity and value of the offer of salvation cannot be understood. The doctrine of retribution is a necessary prerequisite to that of delivering grace. God must be apprehended as a Law-giver and a Judge before he can be known as a Redeemer.

In a general sense, the Old Testament may be said to contain the law, and the New Testament the gospel. They are accordingly contrasted by the apostle (*2 Cor.* 3:6) in respect to the tendencies of the whole, as the letter that kills and the spirit that gives life. The foundations were laid broad and deep and strongly cemented by ages of the continued inculcation of God's essential righteousness.

What is the Old Testament in its grand divisions but the law proclaimed at Sinai, confirmed by the providential retributions of the history, devoutly meditated upon and practised by the psalmists and other inspired poets, and expanded and enforced by the added revelations of the prophets? When the law had, by all these concurrent methods, been worked into the minds and hearts and lives of men, then, and not before, was there an adequate basis on which to rear a superstructure that should match it in amplitude and in solidity – the revelation of God's immeasurable grace.

While, however, the two Testaments are predominantly what has now been described, they are not exclusively so. The statement, though correct in the main, is not exhaustive. The gospel was already witnessed by the law and the prophets (*Rom.* 3:21); and the faith of Christ re-enacts and establishes the law (*Rom.* 3:31). Coupled with the revelation of God's justice under the Old Testament, there was a co-ordinate disclosure of his grace, which was set forth with growing clearness and fulness from the beginning to the end.

Every advance in the presentation of the one was attended or followed by a corresponding advance in the knowledge of the other. Judgement and mercy are concomitants, as well as mutual opposites or rather counterparts, being reverse sides of the same divine excellence. Acts or declarations confirmatory of the one, serve consequently to illustrate and enforce the other. And the two series of progressive and related lessons move along together side by side throughout the whole of the former dispensation.

While, however, the gospel was already substantially preached before Christ came, this was prevailingly done in a legal form and under legal aspects. The pardon of sin, for instance, and reconciliation with God, were accomplished by sacrifices, which prefigured, it is true, the atonement of the Son of God, and derived from it all their present efficacy but were nevertheless a ceremonial institution, enacted in the law, to be performed by the offerer himself, and making up a part of his righteousness in view of the law.

Mercy came to him indeed as unmerited grace to an offender, and yet under the form of an acceptance or justification procured by a performance of his own, or an act in whose performance he took part. The mercy that cancels sin did not drop out of sight, but it could not stand forth so conspicuously and in its own proper simplicity as now, when the typical sacrifice has been merged into and superseded by the great reality, and our entire pardon and justifying righteousness are seen to be wrought out by another in our stead.

And so long as the free grace of the gospel was not yet exhibited in its fulness it was also impossible that the law itself, to which the former dispensation was mainly devoted, should attain its complete expression. Dark and threatening as Sinai was, the law never appeared in such majesty, was never enforced by such sanctions, never exerted such a constraining power on men's hearts, and the exceeding breadth of the commandment was never so laid open as in the transaction on Calvary.

We have now to inquire into the particular function assigned to the book of Job in unfolding this blended revelation of law and gospel. One obvious characteristic belonging to it in common with the other poetical books, and in which it stands in marked contrast with the rest of the Old Testament, is that it is occupied with what is individual and personal. The books of Moses contain God's covenant with Israel as a nation. The historical books record his dealings with the people as such. The books of the prophets make known his will to Israel and concerning Israel as the people of God. These set forth the general principles and methods of the divine administration.

The promises and threatenings concern the entire body of the people or some considerable section of them, and individuals share the fortunes of the mass. If prosperous abundance is set upon an obedient people, the wicked among them participate in the benefit. If a nation of transgressors is led into captivity, the calamity involves the righteous with the rest. But Job stands alone and by himself. He is dealt with as an individual, not as one of a certain race or nation, and particularly not as one of the chosen seed or covenant people, to which he does not even belong. In his history we see the righteousness of God in its relations not to Israel, but to an individual man.

The Psalms record the devout meditations and aspirations of pious souls, taking as their theme God's attributes, his word or his works. The Song of Solomon, which celebrates the divine institution of marriage, forms a striking parallel to Psalm 45. Lamentations is properly an appendix to the book of Jeremiah. Leaving these out of view for the present, the other three poetical books are occupied with the righteousness of God as verified in the experience of men. Proverbs exhibits this verification as a fact of ordinary observation. On the whole, and as a general rule, and agreeably to the native tendencies of things, virtue is rewarded and vice is punished.

But general rules have their exceptions. And to the common order of providence as exhibited in Proverbs there are two apparent exceptions. These are so serious in their character, and withal of so frequent occurrence, as to demand attention. There may be prosperity without piety; and there may be piety without prosperity. The first of these is treated in the book of Ecclesiastes. It presents the case of a man of the rarest wisdom, and with every facility that abundant wealth and royal station could supply, who set himself with deliberate purpose to extract gratification from earthly sources, but found that everything was vanity. And after the baffling experiments of a lifetime he came at length to the conclusion that to fear God and keep his commandments was the only way to secure real enjoyment and man's true welfare.

The other exception furnishes the theme of the book of Job. This deals with the case of piety without prosperity, or the righteousness of God as exercised towards pious sufferers. Its lessons all grow out of this theme, or cluster about it. It is here, therefore, that we are to look for that unfolding of doctrine which belongs to it in the system of the Old Testament. The righteousness of God in its more general and obvious manifestations is assumed as the starting-point.

This is taken for granted as well-understood and agreed upon between Job and his friends at the outset. But a crisis occurs in Job's spiritual history in which the opinions that they have hitherto entertained are not adequate. A state of affairs arises which is at variance with their defective notions of the divine righteousness.

In the struggle that ensues, new light is imparted, and more accurate conceptions are reached. God's righteousness had been inadequately apprehended in two respects, belonging severally to the two poles of Old Testament truth or the two phases of Old Testament instruction, the law and the gospel.

The question that agitates the soul of Job is that of his personal relation to God. Is he the object of the divine displeasure, or will God accomplish his salvation? But in fact he knew neither the extent of the divine displeasure nor the greatness of God's salvation. The righteousness of God condemned more in him than he suspected; while that which he looked upon as a sentence of condemnation was a measure of God's grace.

The new impressions which Job gains of the extent and spirituality of the law of God appears from his altered language respecting himself. His oft-repeated assertions of his righteousness, which were even carried to the extent of chiding God as having done him wrong in sending afflictions upon him which he had not deserved, are superseded by penitent confession and self-abhorrence. 'I abhor myself, and repent in dust and ashes' (42:6).

This change was wrought in his mind by the instruction received from Elihu, coupled with God's manifestation of himself. Elihu took the stumbling-block out of his way which had led to his previous false conclusions by showing him that, in inflicting extraordinary sufferings upon him, God was not thereby charging him with unusual guilt.

This cause of offence removed, Job could listen with unprejudiced ear to Elihu's suggestion of a deeper and more spiritual view of the nature of sin, as not merely consisting in actual transgressions such as the friends had linked with God's judgements, but as represented likewise in pride of heart and evil purpose (33:17). With his thoughts thus turned inward, Job finds reasons for the strokes of divine chastisement which he had not previously recognized, and he cannot regard himself with the same complacency as before.

But pious men in the Old Testament nowhere reach the platform of the New in this respect; and it was impossible that they should, because the facts on which the Christian doctrine of the law and of sin is based had not then been made known. This ought to be borne in mind in estimating the language of these ancient saints.

We see them maintain their own righteousness in the view of God, when we would look rather for a humble confession of utter unworthiness. They plead with God to save them for his righteousness' sake, when we would expect to hear them sue instead for unmerited mercy. And we find it hard to enter into their feelings. We can scarcely acquit them of irreverence, or comprehend how such good men can speak as they do.

It is true, and this affords a partial explanation of the matter, that these assertions of their own goodness are mostly made in opposition to avowed or implied charges of criminality of which they are guiltless. The psalmists were often, like Job, the objects of unjust aspersions and slanders; and they were entitled to declare their innocence of what had been falsely alleged against them with honest indignation. But they do not limit themselves to the claim of being pure from that which has been wrongfully attributed to them, nor to the claim of an integrity that should shield them from the censure of men but, while with the same breath confessing their sinfulness, they lay claim to an uprightness of such breadth and purity that it can maintain itself at the bar of God and expect his approbation.

It is also true that in making their appeals to God's righteousness they include under this term his faithfulness as well as his justice. They intend by the righteousness of God that attribute in virtue of which he does right, not merely in view of their deserts, but in view of his own gracious engagements. They remember his covenant and his promises; and the righteousness of God assures them that he will keep that word which he has mercifully given.

But with all these explanations and abatements, we cannot but feel how differently the apostle Paul is accustomed to speak of himself, and what a different estimate he puts upon his own deservings. 'Not by works of righteousness which we have done, but according to His mercy He saved us' (*Titus* 3:5). 'I am carnal, sold under sin . . . For the good that I will to do, I do not do; but the evil I will not to do, that I practice . . . O wretched man that I am! Who will deliver me from this body of death?' (*Rom.*7:14, 19, 24). Such an experience belongs to the New Testament exclusively.

There is repentance in the Old Testament. There are confessions of sin. There are deep views of its greatness and vileness and enormity. There are prayers for forgiveness. There are breathings after greater conformity to the will of God. All the roots of the apostolic experience are there, but they are never quickened into the same intensity of life, never reach the same expansion, they never gain that ascendancy, that complete mastery of the soul, which shapes all its thinking and feeling and makes its constant attitude before God that of helpless unworthiness. And why? They had never learned the lesson of the cross of Christ.

The vastness of that provision first gave an idea of the greatness of the necessity. The demerit of sin was never so plainly seen as in the light of the infinite merit of the atonement which was requisite to efface it. And the utter worthlessness of our own righteousness first became manifest from the fact that men are justified without any worthiness or deservings of their own, by simple trust in the righteousness of another. The full apprehension of this humbling and abasing, yet at the same time elevating and cheering truth altered, of necessity, the whole complexion of piety. It changed the very basis of men's standing in the sight of God, or at least enabled them to see more distinctly than was possible before where they really did stand.

It swept the gathered sand and rubbish from the rock, and precluded the possibility of their imagining that by heaping these together they were adding to the strength of their position or the security of their hope. But this, while it banished forever all thought of any claim or merit or righteousness in the sight of God, gave a new and impregnable basis of confidence before him – a confidence which no craft of Satan and no storms of affliction could disturb.

It is, however, on the side of the gospel that the lessons of the book of Job chiefly lie. These are all in the direction of the ampler disclosures to be subsequently made, though of course they do not in any case pass the bounds imposed on the knowledge of God's grace for the time then present, nor do they ever anticipate in its fulness what was reserved for a brighter future.

Piety was still, as it is prevailingly characterized in the Old Testament, 'the fear of the Lord' (28:28). The love of God, springing from the knowledge and belief of the love that God has to us, had not been made perfect (*1 John* 4:16, 18). In these unfoldings of gospel truth, we are not to expect any direct presentation of the person of the Messiah. He is not in the Old Testament invoked in individual straits or in present necessities. He is ever exhibited rather as the Hope of Israel and the Saviour of the world. His coming was to introduce an era of peace and holiness and bliss. From the existing degeneracy and defection of the people of God, or the calamities by which they were threatened or overwhelmed, from the growing power of their adversaries or the prospect of the downfall of these mighty foes, the prophets pointed forward to him in whose days Judah shall be saved and Israel shall dwell safely, and under whose beneficent reign all nations shall flock to the mountain of the LORD, beating their swords into ploughshares and learning war no more.

But it was not so clear to their minds that this same Saviour was the present deliverer of each one of his people in his own individual distress. Hence suffering saints in the time of their trouble call not upon the name of the Messiah for help and rescue, but upon the name of the LORD, unaware that they are directing their petitions to the same person whose appearance amongst men shall introduce the anticipated glories of the future.

But addressing the LORD as they do in the capacity of their covenanted Redeemer, soliciting from him the help which he alone can supply, making him the sole ground of their confidence as well as of all their affection and desire, it is in fact, if not in form, the Son of God to whom they make their appeal. And all the knowledge that they gain of this divine Saviour, and the homage that they learn to pay to him, and the trust that they repose in him, is a direct preparation for the doctrine of Christ. They knew not at the time that this line of instruction which they were following converged upon that other line which taught them of the Son of David and the King of Israel. The point of junction was visibly reached when the Word was made flesh. Then the divine Redeemer and the expected Saviour were consciously identified[1]; the Lord from heaven to whom each struggling soul had looked for succour, and the son of Abraham in whom all the families of the earth were to be blessed; he who baffled Satan's wiles and rescued Job from his snare, and the seed of the woman who was to crush the serpent's head and restore the fallen race of man.

Additional elements of messianic instruction are found in the typical character of Job and that of Elihu. They are each representative of a class which finds its highest exemplification in Christ. Whether the type was discerned to be such by the writer of this book and his original readers, it might be difficult to determine. But whether it was or not, it supplies an exemplar conformed to the model of him who was afterwards to be revealed.

It presents a character or an office which would be better understood and more correctly appreciated when it was realized in Christ, for its having been known before, exhibited in others. And the idea to which it gives rise is certainly linked with the expected Saviour in other parts of the Old Testament, in a manner which shows that this connection was patent to the inspired penmen themselves.

The typical correspondence between Job as a pious man sorely afflicted and the man of sorrows has been suggested in a former chapter. This is no mere casual relation of accidental resemblance, but rests upon a general principle of the divine administration. It is a principle consistently applied in God's dealings with his children, that they are made perfect through sufferings. It was thus with Job. It has been thus, and will be, with many more in every age. The circumstances and the particular mode of its application may differ greatly, but the law is the same. It was thus with God's own Son when revealed in human flesh. He too 'learned obedience by the things which he suffered and, having been perfected, he became the Author of eternal salvation to all who obey him'

[1]The relation of Job 19:25 to the Messiah is more particularly stated, pp. 103–4.

(*Heb.* 5:8–9). This uniform method of God's grace is especially dwelt upon by the Psalmists, and its highest application is deduced or foreseen by them. On the basis of their own experience of trial, with its resulting benefits to them, and through them to others, they repeatedly (for example, Psalms 6, 69, 71, etc.) portray the righteous man oppressed by calamities. The picture which they draw is mostly a general one, such as has its counterpart in great numbers of God's faithful servants, who, though weak, imperfect, and sinful, have passed through deep waters and found safety in delivering grace.

But sometimes, as in Psalm 22, the picture is an ideal rather than a portrait. The human characteristics are preserved, but the excellencies are heightened till they have become faultless; imperfections are removed till absolute sinlessness is reached; suffering is followed by unbounded exaltation and glory; and the blessed results of the sorrows swell to proportions that admit no limitation of space or time. The picture is plainly human, and yet it transcends all ordinary human experience. It has and can have but one realization: the Holy Sufferer is the incarnate Son of God.

Elihu is himself such a 'messenger' as he describes (33:23–24), 'a mediator, one among a thousand, to show to man His uprightness'. He had been selected from all others and sent of God to expound to Job the divine will and purpose in this mysterious dispensation, and to make known to him his duty in the case. And this was with the result that he had foreshown:

> Then He is gracious to him, and says,
> 'Deliver him from going down to the Pit;
> I have found a ransom' (33:24).

Elihu acts the part of a divinely commissioned and effectual instructor, a teacher who is the instrument of salvation to his suffering and needy friend. He fulfils, in a lower sense, the very function of the great Teacher and Prophet of the LORD, in response to whose prevalent vindication the same reply is given:

'Deliver him from going down to the Pit;
I have found a ransom' (33:24),

only the ransom is then no longer limited to the figurative sense in which Elihu uses it of the sufferer's own improved spiritual state as an adequate ground or reason for his release from further endurance. The great Teacher has provided a ransom in the strict and proper sense for the release of his people, now and forever, from the bondage that oppresses them.

As the book of Job circles about the conflict in which this man of God was engaged, its lessons mainly concern the foe with whom he had to contend on the one hand, and the supports and encouragements vouchsafed to him on the other. His real adversary was not God, as his friends alleged, and as he apprehended, but Satan. And here a new view is opened into the kingdom of darkness. The great foe to human peace and goodness is here for the first time in Scripture disclosed in his proper person and character.

The serpent had tempted Eve; yet though the narrative of the fall requires the assumption of a spiritual agent concerned in the transaction, his presence is not distinctly mentioned, but left to be vaguely inferred. Here, however, he is explicitly named; his spiritual nature, his malignity, his great power, his subtlety, and untiring assiduity of evil are exposed. At the same time, it is shown that he is limited, restrained, and overruled, and good brought out of his evil devices by the gracious providence of God.

This is an important advance toward the fulness of New Testament revelation on this subject, in which a disclosure is made not merely of a single adversary, but of the whole hierarchy of evil, embracing principalities, powers, and multitudes of spirits of wickedness. There a broader view is afforded of the territory covered by the conflict and of the method in which it is conducted, as well as a heightened assurance of victory over foes already vanquished by the Captain of our salvation, and who shall be bruised under the feet of each of his people shortly.

We see in Job how his afflictions were a test of the sincerity and strength of his pious fear, and how his confidence in God's righteousness carried him successfully through; how he clung to his belief, in spite of all outward appearances, that God was faithful and would not desert his servant, and how at length he learned that affliction might be converted into a benefit.

But the disciple of Christ has a firm support and a wealth of consolation altogether new, in the assurance afforded him of the infinite love of God. 'He who did not spare His own Son, but delivered Him up for us all, how shall He not with Him also freely give us all things?' (_Rom. 8:32_). All things are yours, death as well as life, sorrow as well as joy. In tribulation, distress, and persecution, 'we are more than conquerors through Him who loved us. For I am persuaded that neither death nor life, nor angels nor principalities nor powers, nor things present nor things to come, nor height nor depth, nor any other created thing, shall be able to separate us from the love of God which is in Christ Jesus our Lord' (_Rom._ 8:37–39).

In this consciousness the child of God glories in tribulation, assured that he shall be kept from real harm by his heavenly Father, knowing that sorrow is one of the appointed agencies of grace, since tribulation produces perseverance, character and hope that does not disappoint (_Rom._ 5:4–5); looking unto Jesus, and rejoicing to be conformed to him who endured the cross, despising the shame (_Heb._ 12:2). Hence the striking difference between the demeanour of the apostles and followers of Christ under calamity and that of the saints of God in the Old Testament.

The moans and complaints of desertion, which are uniformly heard from the latter in times of sore distress, grow directly out of the legal aspect under which they contemplated the character of God. But outward distress never brings a shadow over the spirits of the apostles. It is to them no token of the divine displeasure, but is rather hailed as an evidence of sonship. It is the love of God which sends affliction, which supports under affliction, and which delivers out of affliction.

The gospel reveals also, as it was never apprehended before, the heavenly inheritance, that far more exceeding and eternal weight of glory, with which the sufferings of this present time are not worthy to be compared. Job was brought in his conflict into contact with the doctrine of immortality; but he only attained a limited conception of this blessed truth and never drew from it that abundant comfort and solace which, when rightly understood, it is adapted to supply. His confidence that God would not forever withhold his favour from him, coupled with the fact that there was no room left for that favour to display itself in the present life, had driven him to the conclusion that it must be granted to him in the world to come.

He laid hold of his immortality to steady himself in the absence of any earthly hope. It never occurred to him to prefer it to every earthly hope, even if this latter had been possessed in the fullest measure. Life without God's favour and blessing would not indeed have been an object of desire to him any more than to the psalmist, who exclaims in Psalm 73:25:

Whom have I in heaven *but You*?
And *there is* none upon earth *that* I desire besides You.

But life with God's favour was his chief inheritance and his portion. The idea had not presented itself to his mind that the boundless hereafter blessed with God's presence was a more desirable portion than this brief life could be with the same divine presence and blessing. He had faith that God would vindicate his servant and appear upon his side in the future state. But he had not so far surmounted the gloom of the grave and the shadowy nature of the world of spirits as to transport into it the full conception of a life with God, a life free from sin and every form of sorrow, a glory and bliss eternal. It was not until the divine Saviour had himself appeared, and the magnitude of redemption and its unending results had in consequence been disclosed, that men could say with the apostle Paul, that though to live was Christ, yet to die was gain (*Phil.* 1:21).

The sense of immortality to which Job attained was likewise echoed by the psalmists, who speak upon occasion of the future life, but in ambiguous and doubtful phrases, which leave it uncertain how clear their conceptions may have been.

The prophets reached the same result by a somewhat different route. God's covenant faithfulness to Israel secured his people as a whole in all perpetuity against death and destruction; or if their fortunes were so broken that they seemed dead and buried, he would accomplish their resurrection. And this deliverance from death and from all the evils resulting from the fall, which was guaranteed to the body as a whole, was secured likewise to its constituent members.

But these flashes of assurance which we find in the Old Testament are as nothing compared with the clear and steady light shed on the future life in the New Testament. And this fulness of revelation has revolutionized the whole idea and aim of life. The believer has learned to regard the transient present as of small account in comparison with the eternity that lies before him, to 'Set [his] mind on things above, not on things on the earth'(*Col.* 3:2), to 'lay up . . . treasures in heaven' (*Matt.* 6:20), and not to 'look at the things which are seen but at the things which are not seen. For the things which are seen *are* temporary, but the things which are not seen *are* eternal' (*2 Cor.* 4:18). With such a blissful portion in prospect, what is all the 'light affliction, which is but for a moment' (*2 Cor.* 4:17) to which he can be subjected here?

REAL LASTING HAPPINESS

2: The Doctrine of Immortality in the Old Testament

There is a broad and palpable distinction between Old and New Testament saints in their attitude relative to the future life. And the desire to exhibit this sharply and strongly may perhaps have led to the employment of language that is capable of being misunderstood or misinterpreted. In what has been said upon this subject in this volume there is no disposition to deny or overlook the fact that from the very beginning of the old economy the immortality of the soul and a future state of unending existence were revealed and were believed.

The indications of this are clear. This was a common doctrine throughout the ancient world. The very heathen had some notion, though vague and incorrect, of a life hereafter. This truth is involved in the account of man's creation, who alone of all terrestrial beings was made in God's image (*Gen.*1:27), and whose soul, breathed into him by the LORD, is expressly distinguished from his material body (*Gen.* 2:7;

compare *Eccles.* 12:7). It is also involved in the account of the tree of life in the Garden of Eden, and in the law there given rewarding obedience with life and making death the penalty of transgression (see *Prov.* 3:18; 8:35, 36; 12:28; 14:27; 15:24), as well as in the promise of redemption from the damage of the Fall (*Gen.* 3:15, compare *Isa.* 25:8; 26:19).

It is explicitly recognized in the translation of Enoch (*Gen.* 5:24), as also subsequently in that of Elijah (*2 Kings* 2:1), and in the reappearance of Samuel (*1 Sam.* 28:14). It is also found in the expression used of the deceased patriarchs and others, 'gathered to his people' (*Gen.* 25:8), or 'gathered to their fathers' (*Judg.* 2:10), which is clearly distinguished from their burial, and must therefore relate not to their bodies laid in the ancestral tomb but to their joining those who had gone before them, in the world of spirits.

It is included in the special term 'Sheol' (*2 Sam.* 22:6), employed to designate the region of the dead, which is obscured in the common English version by being sometimes translated 'the grave' or 'pit' and sometimes 'hell', though it denotes neither the place of interment nor the place of future torment, but the common location of departed spirits, into which all men pass at death. When Isaiah (14:9–27) represents the mighty dead in Sheol as taunting the deceased monarch of Babylon with his downfall, the language is no doubt figurative; but it is based upon and lends its sanction to the current doctrine of a continued, conscious, and intelligent existence after death.

Possibly, an intelligence beyond that which is possessed in this world may be ascribed to the departed (*Job* 28:22), where the wisdom that is 'hidden from the eyes of all living' is said to have been at least heard of by 'destruction and death', that is, by those who people the realm over which death holds sway.

The burial of the bodies of the dead, instead of burning them or disposing of them in some other way, is a token that in the popular belief they were still regarded as a part of the person, and were not to be destroyed, but preserved in anticipation of a future resurrection. And the explicit directions given by Jacob (*Gen.* 49:29) and by Joseph (*Gen.* 50:24–25), that their bodies should be taken to the land of Canaan, seems to indicate the interpretation which they put upon the promise so often repeated, 'For all the land which you see I give to you and your descendants forever' (*Gen.* 13:15; 35:12), as pledging to them a personal share in the actual possession of that land, or at least of what was typified and represented by it. They, as well as their seed, have the assurance of a part in the ultimate accomplishment; so that the representation made in Hebrews 11:13–16, of the faith of the patriarchs, is amply sustained.

When further the LORD calls himself (*Exod.* 3:6) 'the God of Abraham, the God of Isaac, and the God of Jacob', this establishes or recognizes a relation, which, as our Saviour expounds (*Matt.* 22:32), and as all must have felt, could not be limited to this life, but must have spread itself over the entire future of their being. To which may be added that the popular belief is reflected likewise in the impious arts of necromancers, and in the criminal conduct of those who resorted to them (*1 Sam.* 28:7, 8; *Isa.* 8:19). And what is thus already taught in the very beginning of the Old Testament is repeated and enlarged in the communications subsequently made through the psalmists and the prophets.

Still, though these things are true, and in a just view of the Old Testament should not be lost sight of, the wide chasm remains between those who preceded and those who followed the advent of the Son of God. The completed doctrine of Christ and the greatness of the redemption which he achieved, his own actual return from the state of the dead, and his ascension to heaven as the forerunner and type of his people, opened a new view and poured fresh light upon the mystery of the world to come; and abundant springs of consolation, previously untasted, gushed forth for suffering and tempted souls.

All the instructions previously given were in comparison vague, obscure, and indistinct. Both in the promises of God and in the hopes of the people, this life had been emphasized rather than the next. The present life was prominently held up and looked to as the sphere both of duty and of enjoyment. The first thing to be learned, and that to which the early lessons of revelation and of divine disciplinary training were devoted, was the significance of a life with God here as a life of faith and obedience. Men were taught to sanctify their present activity and present experiences. If these were duly attended to, the future might be safely left with God, even though few explicit disclosures had been made concerning it.

The proper conception of a life with God on earth was the only basis on which it was possible to construct a correct idea of a life with God in heaven. The former truth was first inculcated, therefore, as a necessary preliminary to any just apprehension of the latter. The mere continuance of spiritual being is a philosophical doctrine, not a religious truth. An immortality without God is devoid of all reality or significance, and falls to the level of the pagan notion, which is as far as possible from all that is taught us in the Word of God.

Hence, though the germs of the gospel doctrine of a blessed immortality are traceable everywhere in the Old Testament, the power of this truth was not apprehended, nor were all its relations perceived. It is with this, as with much beside, for example, the deity of the Messiah, which was known and distinctly declared, and yet no such place was assigned to it in the system of truth as is given to it in the New Testament, and as we now see properly belongs to it. So with the doctrine of immortality, the ancient saints did not recur to it in trouble, nor draw from it the manifold consolation which it is capable of supplying. They did not apply it to the solution of the perplexed problems of God's providence. They did not go forth to it in glad anticipation, and fix their hopes upon it as their chief and highest portion.

The aged patriarchs indeed anticipate their departure with composure, and lay themselves down peacefully to die. There is no lamentation in the prospect of this inevitable event, no regrets at leaving the world, no wish expressed that they might live longer. The moans and complaints of Job and the psalmists are invariably uttered under a sense of desertion. They are under a cloud as they seem to themselves to be going down to death. They interpret the providence which threatens their dissolution as the withdrawal of God's favour. This is the secret of their gloom, not that they must die, but that God is alienated from them. If so, they are without hope; they are ruined here and hereafter. Hence their dismal complaints.

But where is there, even from the most favoured of these ancient worthies, a clear, outspoken testimony like that of the apostle Paul as he neared the end of his earthly career? 'For I am already being poured out as a drink offering, and the time of my departure is at hand . . . Finally, there is laid up for me the crown of righteousness, which the Lord, the righteous Judge, will give to me on that Day, and not to me only but also to all who have loved his appearing' (*2 Tim.* 4:6, 8).

SOME OTHER
BANNER OF TRUTH
TITLES

SERMONS ON JOB
John Calvin

Calvin preached on the Book of Job on weekdays in 1554–5. These sermons abound in faithful and lively exposition and remain among the finest examples of evangelical preaching. A quality facsimile reproduction of Arthur Golding's translation of the sermons first published in 1574.

ISBN: 0 85151 644 0
784 pp. Cloth-bound £34.95/$69.99

ALL THINGS FOR GOOD
Thomas Watson

In this fine study of Romans 8:28, Watson explains how both the best and the worst experiences work for the good of God's people.

ISBN: 0 85851 478 2
128 pp. Paperback £2.50/$4.99

A LIFTING UP FOR THE DOWNCAST
William Bridge

Depression is not unique to our times. To encourage the depressed, Bridge wrote this choice book and filled it with the kind of rich encouragement which our generation too rarely hears.

ISBN: 0 85151 298 4
288 pp. Paperback £3.50/$7.50

PRECIOUS REMEDIES AGAINST SATAN'S DEVICES
Thomas Brooks

Brooks treated the seductive influence and terrible power of Satan in a way 'greatly more full and suggestive than in the literature of the present day'.

ISBN: 0 85151 002 7
256 pp. Paperback £3.50/$7.50

OTHER OLD TESTAMENT EXPOSITIONS:

GENESIS
John Calvin
ISBN: 0 85151 093 0, £19.95/$39.99

LEVITICUS
Andrew Bonar
ISBN: 0 85151 086 8, £12.95/$25.99

JUDGES
A. R. Fausset
ISBN: 0 85151 762 5, price pending

PSALMS
David Dickson
ISBN: 0 85151 481 2, £19.95/$35.99

PSALMS
W. S. Plumer
ISBN: 0 85151 209 7, £27.95/$59.99

PSALM 119 (3 volumes)
Thomas Manton
ISBN: 0 85151 576 2, £35.95/$79.99

PSALM 119
Charles Bridges
ISBN: 0 85151 176 7, £10.95/$24.99

PROVERBS
Charles Bridges
ISBN: 0 85151 088 4, £13.95/$25.99

ECCLESIASTES
Charles Bridges
ISBN: 0 85151 322 0, £9.95/$19.99

SONG OF SOLOMON
James Durham
ISBN: 0 85151 352 2, £11.95/$23.99

JEREMIAH & LAMENTATIONS
John Calvin
Set of five volumes:
ISBN: 0 85151 552 5, £49.95/$109.99

EZEKIEL
William Greenhill
ISBN: 0 85151 669 6, £21.95/$44.99

DANIEL
John Calvin
ISBN: 0 85151 092 2, £16.95/$35.99

DANIEL
E. J. Young
ISBN: 0 85151 154 6, £13.95/$27.99

JONAH
Hugh Martin
ISBN: 0 85151 115 5, £9.95/$18.99

HOSEA
John Calvin
ISBN: 0 85151 473 1, £10.95/$22.99

JOEL, AMOS & OBADIAH
John Calvin
ISBN: 0 85151 474 X, £10.95/$22.99

JONAH, MICAH & NAHUM
John Calvin
ISBN: 0 85151 475 8, £10.95/$22.99

HABAKKUK, ZEPHANIAH & HAGGAI
John Calvin
ISBN: 0 85151 477 4, £9.95/$21.99

ZECHARIAH & MALACHI
John Calvin
ISBN: 0 85151 476 6, £12.95/$26.99

For free illustrated catalogue please write to:
THE BANNER OF TRUTH TRUST
3 Murrayfield Road, Edinburgh EH12 6EL
P O Box 621, Carlisle, Pennsylvania 17013, U S A